Without Spanking or Spoiling

A Practical Approach to Toddler and Preschool Guidance

Second Edition

By Elizabeth Crary

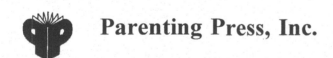 **Parenting Press, Inc.**

Copyright © 1979, 1993
All rights reserved
Printed in the United States of America

First Edition, Seventeen Printings
Second Edition

"The Difficult Child" and "The Easy Child" from *Your Child Is a Person*
by Dr. Stella Chess, Dr. Alexander Thomas, and Dr. Herbert G. Birch
Copyright © 1965 by Dr. Stella Chess, Dr. Alexander Thomas, and Dr. Herbert G. Birch
All rights reserved. Reprinted with permission from Viking Penguin, Inc.

ISBN 978-0-943990-74-3
LC 92-085497

Parenting Press, Inc.
814 North Franklin Street
Chicago, Illinois 60610
www.ParentingPress.com

Table of Contents

Introduction

Every parent has heard the phrase "spare the rod; spoil the child." And most parents have heard someone say that spanking is a form of child abuse. Parents often ask, *"Is it really possible to raise children without spanking or spoiling them?"* The good news is, ***"Yes! You can raise children without spanking or spoiling."*** Children who do not receive clear limits are often spoiled; however, spanking is only one way to establish limits. There are so many other choices!

With some children the task of child rearing is relatively simple. The child is born with an easy temperament, and the parent has useful parenting skills. In other situations, either the child is more challenging, or the tools the parent has don't work well for that child. In these cases, parents, stepparents, daycare providers, and teachers need to work together.

Without Spanking or Spoiling offers 32 alternatives to spanking, over 150 tips to solving the most common behavior problems, 10 summary sheets, and a 5-step problem solving process. This material can be used to gain a better understanding of child guidance in general, or to resolve a particular issue. For either purpose, start by reading Chapters One and Two. These chapters give you information you can use to make all the techniques you use more effective. As you read the other chapters mark the tools that particularly appeal to you. Exercises are provided to help make the material more relevant. The way you use these tools depends on your values, your experience, and your child's personality.

To alter a specific behavior, refer to the problem solving planning sheet on page 103 and follow the steps. You will come up with a variety of ideas. If you have trouble filling in the blanks you can refer to the text or Appendix One for ideas. In most cases, using the problem solving process will generate many ideas. When you evaluate ideas keep in mind your long-term goals for your child, as well as your child's developmental level and temperament. Occasionally parents find a conflict between their short-term convenience and their long-term goals. This might happen, for example, if a parent wants her son to be independent (particularly to cook and care for himself) and also likes a clean kitchen.

Many parents find that techniques that worked well with their first child do not help with their second, or that techniques which are effective with young children stop working as those children grow older. When successful techniques lose their effectiveness, parents become frustrated and wonder if something is wrong with them or with their children. When this happens, return to the problem solving sheet and find more alternatives. When parents have a number of techniques available, it is easier to find an approach that meets both their needs and the needs of their growing children.

Every family is special. Each person grows at his or her own rate. Your family may have different needs, and face different challenges from the family across the street. And your child probably does not react the same as all of your friends' children. Your child may be more sensitive, or more challenging, or more persistent than the what you expected, or what you have seen in other children. Whatever your situation, you have plenty of choices. I hope that you will use *Without Spanking or Spoiling* to develop your own effective, loving style of parenting.

Chapter 1: Before You Begin

This book is designed to help make the time parents and children spend together more enjoyable for both. One of the basic principles of human relationships is that you can change only yourself; however, when you change yourself, you change the relationship and the other person must respond somehow. Child guidance is the art of changing your actions so that you increase the probability of getting the behavior you desire.

Without Spanking or Spoiling presents information from several different approaches to child guidance: Parent Effectiveness Training, Behavior Modification, Transactional Analysis, and the Adlerian-Dreikurs approach. The advantage of this book is that all the material presented is appropriate for use with toddlers and preschoolers. All the examples and exercises illustrate the use of these techniques with small children. There is a lot of information presented, but it needs thought and work on your part to put the ideas into action guiding your child. For persons interested in reading more about specific techniques, suggested readings are included at the end of each chapter.

The three-legged stool

Child guidance is like a three-legged stool. To be most effective, the stool needs three supports. The supports are: (1) knowledge of your personal *values*, (2) reasonable *expectations* for your children, and (3) *self acceptance*. If any support is missing, the stool will wobble. We will look briefly at each support below.

First, parents need to know what they value for themselves and for their children. When parents do not know what they want, they often feel dissatisfied without knowing why. Clarifying values helps parents distinguish between long-term and short-term goals. Also, if parents have no clear idea what they want, it is impossible to develop a plan to obtain it.

Second, knowledge of what the parent wants (or values) needs to be tempered by what is possible for the child. Children's behavior varies greatly, both between children of the same age, and between different ages for the same child. Without realistic expectations for his child, a parent may waste much time and energy attempting the impossible, and discourage both the parent and the child in the process.

Finally, parents are more effective when they feel good about themselves. This involves learning how to motivate themselves and taking time to enjoy themselves. When people enjoy themselves, it is easier to enjoy someone else.

This book is divided into seven chapters. Each chapter presents information and exercises on one general topic. The remainder of this chapter presents additional information on the three support skills: recognizing your values, developing reasonable expectations for your child, and encouraging self-esteem. The second chapter offers one way to approach difficult problems. The next four chapters of the book present a variety of techniques for meeting the changing needs of both the growing parent and the growing child. The last chapter integrates the information in the earlier chapters to help you solve problems. Appendix One lists ideas for ten common parenting issues that you can adapt for your concerns. Appendix Two summarizes some of the techniques.

Recognizing your values

Parents are more effective when they know what they value for themselves and how those values influence what they want for their children. Knowing your goals for your child helps you decide whether or not to intervene in her behavior. Understanding your values also helps make you aware when one value conflicts with another. For example, if you have a long-term goal of independence for your child, and a short-term desire for personal convenience, you will think twice when your two-and-a-half-year old son wants to help make scrambled eggs. If you clarify your beliefs while your child is still young, it gives you a chance to bring your actions in line with your beliefs. And children often learn most readily through imitation.

Values are the beliefs or attitudes that motivate people. They are the concepts each person feels are important for himself and possibly for humanity as a whole. For a value to be truly yours, you must act on it — not just verbalize it or think that you should follow it.

Values are completely individual. The attitudes and behaviors that are important to one person may be completely unimportant to another person. As people grow, their values often change. Some values become less important as people incorporate new values into their lives. The variations in values can be most clearly seen when people discuss controversial topics.

Before continuing, it would be helpful for you to take a look at your own values. Two exercises are included. The first focuses on desirable traits in children, and the second involves ranking the traits you think are important.

Exercise 1-1: Desirable Children's Traits
Exercise 1-2: Ranking Children's Traits

Values change with time. Change occurs with both personal beliefs and with the traits you value in your children. You will probably find that what you value for your children changes over time. This happens both because you are changing *and* because your expectations change for children of different ages. For example, you may find intense curiosity in a one year old cute, but the same behavior in a five year old rude. Also, when a one year old says "no-no" and runs away, it may not be as maddening as when the child is three. It is often helpful to redo Exercise 1-2 every year or two to see if your values for your children have changed.

Some values conflict with others. Look at the children's traits you chose. Which were most important to you? Do any of them conflict with each other? Some conflicts are obvious, such as frugality and generosity, or obedience and independence. However, some conflicts are more subtle, such as curiosity and self-control, honesty and politeness, or being popular and standing up for one's own beliefs.

Exercise 1-1: Desirable Children's Traits

INSTRUCTIONS: *Imagine that you have just completed adoption procedures and find that the preschool child you are about to adopt has the characteristics listed below.*

Mark your reaction to each statement listed below.
O=outraged, C=concerned, N=neutral, P=pleased, E=elated

Your child:	responses:	O	C	N	P	E
1. is very active, always on the go.						
2. takes whatever s/he wants.						
3. can throw & catch a ball very well.						
4. is a very beautiful child.						
5. has a smile for everyone.						
6. doesn't want to be dirty or messy.						
7. can do "physical" things easily (i.e., run, climb, ride a trike).						
8. faces unpleasant situations (i.e., doctor's shots) without flinching.						
9. asks questions about everything.						
10. can do things a variety of ways.						
11. always turns out lights when leaving a room.						
12. gives toys away to anyone who asks.						
13. sees what needs to be done and helps without being asked.						
14. tells the truth even when it is to his or her disadvantage.						
15. always wants to do things by self.						
16. is tested as academically gifted.						
17. does what anyone says.						
18. lets another child bite him or her.						
19. doesn't like activities interrupted.						
20. always thanks people.						
21. is always sought out by playmates.						
22. says prayers every night.						
23. can be trusted to leave tempting items alone.						
24. comforts a sad child at preschool.						
25. gets own snack whenever hungry.						

Exercise 1-2: Ranking Children's Traits

INSTRUCTIONS: Rank the personality traits listed below. Begin with 1 as the most important to you. **Note:** *The traits are the same as were presented in Exercise 1-1. The numbers in parentheses indicate the corresponding statement in Exercise 1-1.*

_____ **Active**, lots of energy, always moving (1)
_____ **Aggressive**, competitive (2)
_____ **Athletic**, does well in sports (3)
_____ **Attractive**, physically nice-looking (4)
_____ **Cheerful**, pleasant, friendly (5)
_____ **Clean**, neat, uncluttered (6)
_____ **Coordinated**, physically coordinated (7)
_____ **Courageous**, stands up for own beliefs (8)
_____ **Curious**, inquisitive (9)
_____ **Flexible**, resourceful, innovative (10)
_____ **Frugal**, conserves resources and energy (11)
_____ **Generous**, shares with others (12)
_____ **Helpful to others**, altruistic (13)
_____ **Honest**, truthful (14)
_____ **Independent**, self-reliant (15 & 25)
_____ **Intelligent**, intellectual (16)
_____ **Obedient**, compliant (17)
_____ **Passive**, not aggressive (18)
_____ **Persistent**, "finishing power" (19)
_____ **Polite**, well mannered (20)
_____ **Popular**, liked by peers (21)
_____ **Religious**, respects God (22)
_____ **Self-controlled**, self-restraint (23)
_____ **Sensitive**, considerate of other's feelings (24)

Conflicting values create confusion for small children if they are not clarified. For example, if you tell your daughter to be honest, but fib about her age to get a discount, she will likely decide that thrift is more important than honesty. If you value both obedience and independence, you will need to clarify in what areas the child is to be obedient and where he may be independent. In our family, for instance, there are two areas where obedience is expected: (1) health and safety matters (i.e., "Don't run into the street"), and (2) respect for human life (i.e., "People are not for hitting").

Clarifying behavioral expectations

Most new parents have little, if any, experience with small children. Even people who have younger brothers and sisters, or who did a lot of babysitting find it hard to remember what children do at different ages. This is particularly true with babies and toddlers. It is also important for parents to realize that children vary both in developmental level (the number of skills they possess) and temperamental characteristics (the way they view or respond to the world).

Inappropriate expectations cause anxieties. Many times parents become upset because their child does not do things according to the parents' timetable. For example, one woman became very upset with her 11- month-old son because

Exercise 1-3: Developmental Quiz

INSTRUCTIONS: Decide at what age most children display each trait or ability listed below. Compare your answers with the developmental chart on the next page.

_____ 1. pedals a tricycle

_____ 2. gives his/her first and last name

_____ 3. builds a tower of 4 cubes

_____ 4. says three words other than "mama" and "dada"

_____ 5. dresses without supervision

_____ 6. scribbles spontaneously

_____ 7. uses a spoon, spilling little

---

he would not walk alone. She was afraid he was becoming a "Momma's boy." She was much relieved to find that only about half of the children can walk independently by one year, and that she should not worry until after 14 months which is when most toddlers walk alone. If you can clarify your developmental expectations for your child, it is easier to check your accuracy. Exercise 1-3 reviews your knowledge of skills which develop in the first five years.

Exercise 1-3: Developmental Quiz

Children learn at different rates. A child who sits early will probably walk early, but not necessarily talk early. (Children often appear to "lose" a skill while they concentrate on learning a new one.) One difficulty with many developmental charts is that you don't know whether the ages given are when the skill usually *first appears*, when the *average child* performs the skill, or when *most children* perform the skill. A developmental chart is provided (page 12) which gives an "age window" for some behavioral skills. The window begins when 25% of the children show the skill, changes to shading at the 50% position, ends the shading at the 75% position, and stops when 90% of children perform the skill. Look at your estimated ages on Exercise 1-3 and check them with the age given by the developmental chart for the 75% level and write it down by your answer. You can also get information about how children behave and what they do by attending a parent-toddler class, volunteering in a preschool, or by having other children in your home. It is important to remember that many children act differently at home and visiting so you may need to see children over a period of time to judge their developmental level.

Perfecting a skill takes time. There is often a lag between the beginning, when the skill is noticed, and when the skill is perfected. There is also a lag between the development of a skill and an "associated skill." For example, children can walk up stairs about two months before they can walk down stairs,

Developmental Chart

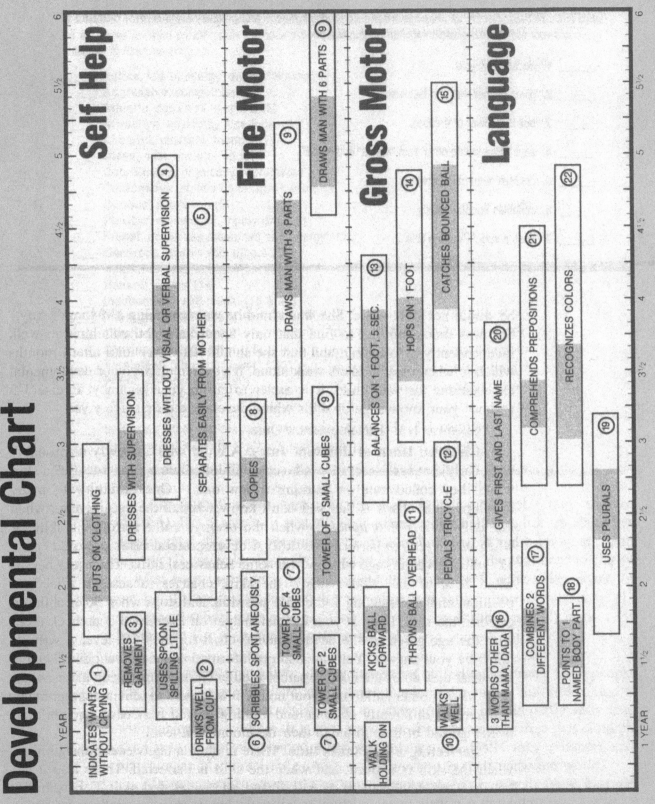

Self Help

- ① INDICATES WANTS WITHOUT CRYING
- PUTS ON CLOTHING
- ③ REMOVES GARMENT
- USES SPOON SPILLING LITTLE
- DRESSES WITH SUPERVISION
- ② DRINKS WELL FROM CUP
- ④ DRESSES WITHOUT VISUAL OR VERBAL SUPERVISION
- ⑤ SEPARATES EASILY FROM MOTHER

Fine Motor

- ⑥ SCRIBBLES SPONTANEOUSLY
- ⑦ TOWER OF 2 SMALL CUBES
- ⑦ TOWER OF 4 SMALL CUBES
- ⑧ COPIES
- ⑨ TOWER OF 8 SMALL CUBES
- DRAWS MAN WITH 3 PARTS
- ⑨ DRAWS MAN WITH 6 PARTS

Gross Motor

- WALK HOLDING ON
- KICKS BALL FORWARD
- ⑩ WALKS WELL
- ⑪ THROWS BALL OVERHEAD
- ⑫ PEDALS TRICYCLE
- ⑬ BALANCES ON 1 FOOT, 5 SEC.
- ⑭ HOPS ON 1 FOOT
- ⑮ CATCHES BOUNCED BALL

Language

- ⑯ 3 WORDS OTHER THAN MAMA, DADA
- ⑱ POINTS TO 1 NAMED BODY PART
- ⑰ COMBINES 2 DIFFERENT WORDS
- ⑲ USES PLURALS
- ⑳ GIVES FIRST AND LAST NAME
- ㉑ COMPREHENDS PREPOSITIONS
- ㉒ RECOGNIZES COLORS

1 YEAR 1½ 2 2½ 3 3½ 4 4½ 5 5½ 6

Instructions for Developmental Chart

INSTRUCTIONS: Outer rectangle begins when 25% of children demonstrate the skill and ends when 90% do. The inner rectangle begins when 50% of children demonstrate skill and ends when 75% do. The circled number indicates additional explanation of item.

Percentage of children demonstrating skill	25%	50%	75%	90%

1. Can child indicate wants without whining or crying? May point, pull or make a pleasant sound.

2. Child should use regular cup or glass without spout.

3. Garment includes pajamas, pants, shirt, but not diapers, hat or socks.

4. Can child put on jeans, shirt, dress, socks without help, except for snaps, buttons or buckles?

5. Does child react calmly when left with strangers or babysitters (no crying, whimpering, or hanging on parent)?

6. Does child scribble spontaneously when given a pencil and paper? (No guiding hand or demonstrating.)

7. Small blocks about 1 inch cube, less than 2 inch cube.

8. Show child a drawn circle. Say "draw a picture just like this one." Any enclosed form passes (i.e., ⊙ ⊘ ⊘). A continuous round motion or unclosed form does not pass (i.e., ∂ ⌇).

9. Say to child "Draw a man." Do not give further instructions. Do not ask or remind about missing parts. When counting number of parts, count each pair as one (i.e., eyes, arms, legs, etc.).

10. Is child able to walk all the way across a large room without falling or wobbling from side to side?

11. Can child throw a ball overhand towards your stomach or chest from a distance of 5 feet (not side arm)?

12. Can child pedal at least ten feet?

13. How long can child balance on one foot without holding on to anything? (Give three chances.)

14. Have child hop several times without holding on to anything.

15. Can child catch a small ball with hands only? (Small ball, the size of tennis ball.)

16. Can child say three specific words which mean the same thing each time they are used (other than "mama" and "dada").

17. Can child put two words together when he speaks? Like "want water" or "play ball." ("Thank you" and "bye-bye" do not count.)

18. Can child point to at least part of his body (hair, eyes, mouth, arms)? Child should know parts well enough to answer stranger without coaching.

19. Does child put an s at the end of words when he is talking about more than one item, like shoes, toys, or cookies?

20. Without coaching can your child say his first and last name clearly? (Answer "no" if child gives first name only or if name is not clear.)

21. Get a chair and a paper. Give your child the following directions. Do not gesture (point or look) to give the child directions. "Put the paper on the chair," "Put the paper behind the chair," "Put the paper in front of the chair," and "Put the paper under the chair." Was the child correct 3 of 4 times?

22. Get four identical items of the colors below. Give the child the following directions (substituting the appropriate word for "item"): "Point to the red item. Point to the yellow item. Point to the green item. Point to the blue item." Did the child get three of the four colors correct without coaching or correcting?

and they can empty things before they can fill them. Exercise 1-4 focuses on some skills on the developmental chart which have associated skills that are accomplished later.

Exercise 1-4: Developmental Lags

Basic temperaments

Children differ from one another in temperamental characteristics. Nine traits have been identified by Drs. Chess, Thomas, and Birch as forming a child's style of behavior. Children were reevaluated periodically, and at each age children showed a clear pattern of individuality. These traits may be inborn or may be developed very early in life. As children grow older, they may change. However, in their study, most of the children continued to exhibit many of the qualities they had shown when they were young. In other children, the changes in behavior style seemed to reflect parental handling or special experiences. A brief description of the nine temperamental characteristics is presented in Exercise 1-5.

Exercise 1-5: Temperamental Characteristics

The particular combination of temperamental characteristics a child has affects the child's acceptability to his or her parents in two ways. First, most parents consciously or unconsciously have a mental picture of what they want their child to be like. It is easier to accept a child who conforms to our image of what a child should be than one who does not. Second, there are certain combinations of personality traits that are almost guaranteed to drive any parent up the wall. It is difficult to remain accepting of a child who is irregular, adapts slowly, reacts intensely, and has a negative mood.

It is possible to modify the basic temperamental characteristics, but it takes patience and consistency over a number of years. On the next two pages are two examples from *Your Child is a Person* by Drs. Chess, Thomas, and Birch. They illustrate how parental handling can affect both a "difficult" child and an "easy" child. Their book also suggests different ways to handle common situations depending on the child's temperament.

The difficult child

Jane and Tommy kept their respective mothers constantly on the go. Their likes and dislikes were never in doubt. They either howled *long* and loudly, or they beamed and chuckled and laughed. Their first reaction to a new situation, however, was generally a negative one. They screamed every time there was a change of routine. It took them both an enormously long time to accept any changes.

They were hard babies to care for in other ways as well. Nothing seemed to go the same way from day to day. One could not predict their naptimes, nor how much they would want to eat or when. In fact, it wasn't even possible to prophesy what their reactions to people and places might be from day to day. They were intense, preponderantly negative in mood, irregular, and slow to adapt.

The two children grew up quite differently. Jane's mother seemed inexhaustibly patient and consistent with her. When Jane was one, two, and even three years old, a denial in the supermarket would turn her into a screaming,

Exercise 1-4: Developmental Lags

INSTRUCTIONS: Look up the average (50%) age for the pairs of skills below.

1. _____ removes garments

   _____ puts clothing on

2. _____ walks holding on

   _____ walks well alone

3. _____ dresses with supervision

   _____ dresses without supervision

4. What personal-social trait appears with the least age variation (smallest window)?

   _____

5. What personal-social trait appears with the greatest age variation (largest window)?

   _____

kicking little fury. But her mother almost never blew up. She would patiently pick Jane off the floor, take the purchases to the check-out counter, and go home without screaming or fussing back at Jane. These tactics were markedly successful, and neighbors were frequently amazed to see the youngster playing contentedly a few minutes later. With proper handling Jane could forget that there had ever been a commotion just as quickly as she could register her howling discontent.

Little by little, as she grew, she became more of a social human being. When, time after time, her violent demands brought firm, consistent, and quiet removal from the social scene, her tantrums diminished. In time they began to look more and more like token attempts at self-assertion. Fortunately, neighbors and relatives took their cues from Jane's parents. They let her scream, but refused to let her inconvenience others. They were pleasant and ungrudging when the child made her lightning switch to positive behavior.

Tommy behaved much like Jane in the beginning. However, his parents reacted to him very differently. They felt harassed from the beginning. When the child's pattern persisted as he passed his first, then his second, and finally his third birthday, they grew increasingly upset. Nothing seemed to satisfy Tommy, even though they were constantly trying to make him happy. They gave in to his demands, reasonable or unreasonable. If he wanted a toy in the supermarket, his mother bought it quickly to avoid trouble. But no matter how much his parents tried to satisfy him, every excursion, every visit, indeed every play period was marked by some commotion. His mother's indulgent attitude had its limits. She

Exercise 1-5: Temperamental Characteristics

How would you rate your child?

1. ACTIVITY LEVEL. How much does your child wiggle and move around when you read to him, at the table, or playing by himself?

active		quiet
1	3	5

2. REGULARITY. Is your child regular about eating times, sleeping times, amount of sleep needed, and bowel movements?

regular		irregular
1	3	5

3. ADAPTABILITY. How quickly does your child adapt to changes in his schedule or routine? How quickly does he adapt to new foods and places?

adapts quickly		slow to adapt
1	3	5

4. APPROACH/WITHDRAWAL. How does your child usually react the first time to new people, new foods, new toys, and new activities?

initial approach		initial withdrawal
1	3	5

5. PHYSICAL SENSITIVITY. How aware is your child of slight noises, slight differences in temperature, differences in taste and differences in clothing?

not sensitive		very sensitive
1	3	5

6. INTENSITY OF REACTION. How strong or violent are his reactions? Does he laugh and cry energetically or does he just smile and fuss mildly?

high intensity		mild reaction
1	3	5

7. DISTRACTIBILITY. Is your child easily distracted or does he ignore distractions? Will he continue to work or play when other noises or children are present?

very distractible		not distractible
1	3	5

8. POSITIVE OR NEGATIVE MOOD. How much of the time does your child show pleasant, joyful behavior compared with unpleasant crying and fussing behavior?

positive mood		negative mood
1	3	5

9. PERSISTENCE. How long does your child continue with one activity? Does he usually continue if it is difficult?

long attention span		short attention span
1	3	5

could take just so much and then would explode, screaming: "You always make trouble. Nobody can satisfy you." She would also make endless threats, but would not carry them out. Tommy's father kept aloof from this frantic interplay between mother and child. One fuss from his son and Daddy left him to his own devices. As time went on there was less and less contact between the two. Both parents were convinced that Tommy was impossible to please or satisfy. Indeed, this had become true, not only at home, but at play and in school.

The easy child Both Greg and Pammy were "good" babies. They slept well, accepted almost every new food without fuss, adjusted to changes in schedules quickly and contentedly. Both children were moderately active and, as they grew older,

Without Spanking or Spoiling

seemed equally happy swinging on the Junglegym or sitting quietly listening to a story. They were models of good behavior even on long automobile trips.

Both children usually welcomed new faces. By the time Greg was three, he played regularly with the neighborhood children, visiting them in their houses and being visited in turn.

To settle the inevitable tussles over toys, his mother and father made clear-cut rules. The child accepted them readily and followed them much as he had accepted and adapted to earlier routines and experiences. He learned quickly that there was a time to share and a time to insist that the toy was his by right. Although he had many ideas for games, he was willing to play his friends' games, too, as his parents had taught him.

Though he had not attended nursery school, he acted like a veteran by the end of the first day in kindergarten. In first grade he made rapid progress in school subjects, eagerly following the teacher's instructions.

Pammy also got along very smoothly with a group of friends when she was three. Usually charming and pleasant, she knew how to take turns on the slide and never threw sand in the sandbox.

Her parents handled her quite differently from the way Greg's had handled him. Pammy's father and mother recalled their own childhoods as unpleasant. They had been constantly chided because whatever they did was not considered good enough — it had to be superlative. They were therefore determined to spare their own child this kind of unhappiness.

When Pammy was a baby, they played with her endlessly and were completely captivated by her cheerful responsiveness. When she was a year old, they found themselves incapable of making the usual first demands: "Don't touch" or "Help put the blocks away." Whenever they tried tentatively to do so, Pammy's charm would always divert them from their purpose.

If Pammy showed her mother a picture she had made, mother's response was always, "Isn't it fun?" If she asked her father to see her perform a new feat in the park, his invariable reaction was, "Wonderful."

Pammy got the impression that everything she did was charming.

The social immaturity had more general adaptive consequences. Thus, on a standardized I.Q. test given her at this time she measured borderline defective. The examining psychologist was sure Pammy didn't score well because she was so busy turning the test into a game that she had never performed what she was asked to do. When she was told to string beads in the manner explained by the tester, Pammy *talked* about beads. "I have beads like these at home. Which beads do you like best?"

When she went to kindergarten she had even more trouble recognizing and following instructions. By second grade she had learned so little about the rules of play that the other children were no longer interested in her.

At seven, although she was still an amiable child, she was beginning to be a lonely one. She was pleasant and wanted to please, but she no longer knew how. Her father's and mother's undiscriminating acceptance of her every move had prevented her from finding out how to work and play when others made the rules or to progress in mastery and responsibility. Her babyish ways are anything but charming now.

Self-acceptance

The third leg of the child guidance "stool" is self-acceptance. For some reason, feeling good about oneself makes working with young children much easier. Most parents have experienced some great days when the sun is shining inside as well as out. Those are the days when everything goes well. Parents have time to watch the ant crawl across the sidewalk or to chase the grasshoppers. Shoes and mittens are easily found, and little milk is spilled. Siblings play surprisingly well together giving the parent a chance to sit and relax or read for a few minutes. Interruptions, when they occur, are gentle or amusing. When parents feel good, they have the internal resources to handle the situations they are facing.

All parents have also experienced bad days when they don't feel well or are under tremendous pressure to get something done. Those are the days when children spill their milk, talk in extremely loud voices, tease their siblings constantly, and can't find their shoes when it is time to go out. When parents feel "low," they have few internal resources to deal with the problems they face.

Most of us would like to have more good days. The simplest way to increase the frequency of pleasant days is to take time to do things you enjoy. When we continually give time, attention and/or support to others, our internal stores are decreased and we begin to run out of patience and understanding. These internal stores can be rebuilt by receiving support or attention from someone else (like a friend) or by doing something enjoyable. Two exercises are included here to help focus on the things you like to do and how you like to use your time.

Exercises 1-6 a & b: My Favorite Things

What you enjoy may surprise you — sometimes pleasantly, sometimes unpleasantly. The insight often promotes change. For example, one woman found that she had a strong need to be alone that she had not been aware of. Her unmet need for solitude led to much frustration with her children. When she occasionally arranged to get a large block of time alone, her irritations decreased. In another case, a father found that there was nothing on his list of favorite things that he did with his children, so he decided to include them in at least one of his favorite activities.

Take time for yourself. Sometimes parents find that it has been a long time since they have done things *they* like to do. Most people need to get away by themselves periodically and do something they enjoy. The activity can be as simple as reading uninterrupted for a couple of hours, or more involved, such as taking a skiing vacation.

Sometimes parents, particularly mothers, feel guilty when they leave their children and go have fun by themselves. They feel that a "good mother" should not want time away from her children. This "good mother" exists only in one's imagination. To be realistic as parents, we need to remember that to be good to our children, we need to be good to ourselves. We are better able to meet our children's needs when we have had our own needs met. Also, if we want our children to have fun, we need to model having fun.

Many people feel they don't have enough time to do all the things they wish to do. Before we can decide whether we have enough time, we need to

Exercise 1-6a: My Favorite Things

INSTRUCTIONS: List ten things you love to do.
Perhaps you may want to consider--
      -your favorite people and what you do with them.
      -your favorite places and what you do there.
      -your favorite possessions and what you do with them.
      -the seasons and what you do during each of them.

1. _____

2. _____

3. _____

4. _____

5. _____

6. _____

7. _____

8. _____

9. _____

10. _____

Exercise 1-6b: Favorite Things, continued

INSTRUCTIONS: Review your responses for Exercise 1-6a and put a (an)
    A by things you like to do **alone**
    P by things you like to do with **people**
    C by things you like to do with **children**
    $ by activities that cost more than **$5** each time you do them
    R by items that involve an element of **risk** (physical or emotional)
    S by things that require a **sitter**

By each response, write the date you last did the activity.

LOOK AT your pattern of responses and complete the sentence below.

I was surprised that _____

_____

_____

look and see what we are doing with the time we have. The next exercise is one way of looking at how people use their time. You may also wish to have your partner or daycare provider do the exercises and talk about how you wish to handle differences that occur.

Exercise 1-7: Time Wheel

You control your time. Once you know how you spend time and how you would like to spend it, you can begin to make changes. Some changes can be made immediately and some need long-range planning. As an example, let us take a look at how the parent in the example of Exercise 1-7 could reallocate her available time. If she wished to spend more time with her husband in the evening, she would need to reduce the size of another segment. She could rearrange time in one of several ways: reduce meal preparation time (by buying some TV dinners or preparing enough for two meals, for example), reduce her time alone by preparing meals instead of reading or sewing, or reducing child care time by hiring a babysitter while she and her husband went out. These are only three of the many possibilities.

A large problem for many people who wish to rearrange their time allocations is child care. Good child care is often costly or difficult to find. One way to overcome both of these limitations is to join or start a babysitting cooperative. Co-ops can be designed to function in the daytime, evenings, weekends, or some combination of them. Several ways to organize babysitting co-ops are suggested in the book *How to Organize a Babysitting Cooperative*, listed below.

In this chapter, we have seen how a person's effectiveness as a parent is influenced by a knowledge of what he values, by his expectations of his child's behavior, and by his feeling of well-being or self-acceptance. These are support skills. They are not directly used at any time; however, they affect all the interactions parents and children have. Additional readings are suggested below for those who wish to read more in these areas. In the next chapter we will look at a procedure parents can use to change behavior problems.

Additional reading

The Second Twelve Months of Life, by Frank and Theresa Caplan. Bantam Books, New York, 1982.
    □ Information about what children are like from ages 1 to 2.
Child Behavior from Birth to Ten, by Frances L. Ilg and Louise Bates Ames. Perennial Library, Harper & Crown, New York, 1982.
    □ Discusses characteristics of different-aged children and how behaviors (i.e., fears, tension outlets, eating habits) typically manifest themselves at different ages.
Your Child is a Person, by Stella Chess, Alexander Thomas, and Herbert G. Birch. The Viking Press, New York, 1965. (Out of print. Check with your library for a copy.)
    □ Discusses basic differences in temperament and how this can affect child-rearing practices.

Exercise 1-7: Time Wheel

EXAMPLE: The circle below represents the 24 hours in a day. Each segment of the circle represents the proportion of time one parent spent in various activities on a typical day.

Sleeping --- 7½ hours
Child care - 6
Chores ----- 2½
    (cooking, washing, etc)
Work ------- 3
Alone ------ 2½ (reading, sewing)
Socializing- 1 (phone, spouse)
Misc. ------- 1½

Part 1. *INSTRUCTIONS: Divide the time circle into segments reflecting how you spend a typical day. (Each mark represents 2 hour.) Then continue with part 2.*

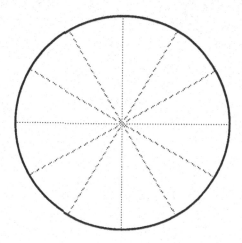

Part 2. *INSTRUCTIONS: Now draw your ideal Time Wheel! How big would you like each segment to be? Then answer the questions to the right of the circle.*

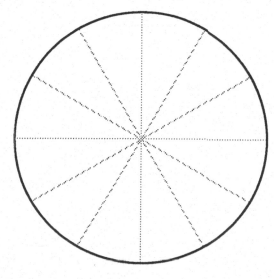

How can you begin to change the size of the segments?

_____

_____

_____

What, specifically, could you do tomorrow or next week to change the size of the time segments?

_____

_____

_____

Your Child's Self-Esteem: The Key to His Life, by Dorothy Corkille Briggs. Doubleday, New York, 1975.
  □ How to help create feelings of self-worth.

How to Organize a Babysitting Cooperative, by Carole Terwilliger Meyers. Carousel Press, Albany, California, 1976.

Pick Up Your Socks ... and other skills growing children need! by Elizabeth Crary. Parenting Press, Seattle, Washington, 1990.
  □ Focuses on teaching children responsibility. Has a chart on what ages children do various household tasks.

Growing Up Again, by Jean Illsley Clarke and Connie Dawson. HarperCollins, New York, 1989.
  □ Provides information and examples of how to give your child self-esteem, even if one did not receive good parenting as a child.

Chapter 2: Steps in Problem Solving

When a problem arises, many parents rush in and solve it in the first way they think of. This approach may solve the problem for the moment, but often causes frustration for one or more of the participants. When the problem is solved this way, it usually is a short-term solution rather than a long-term one. For example, when a parent rushes in and solves a problem for a child, the parent denies that child the opportunity to solve the problem for him or herself. This means that the next time a similar problem occurs, the child will probably expect the parent to solve it again.

This chapter presents five steps for solving behavior problems:
(1) define the problem behaviorally,
(2) gather data,
(3) generate alternatives,
(4) evaluate the alternatives and implement one, and
(5) evaluate the solution.

At first, these steps may be cumbersome and time consuming, but time is saved in the long run because you have to deal with the same problem fewer times. It is not necessary to employ this five-step system for every problem, however it is extremely useful when an unacceptable behavior is persistent or particularly annoying.

ONE: Define the problem behaviorally

Defining the problem behaviorally means deciding specifically what she does or what he says that bothers you. The definition should be clear enough that someone else could look at the child's behavior and *count* the number of times the behavior occurs. Avoid general words (like "bad" or "mean") and personality traits (like "lazy," "rude," "stupid," or "irresponsible"). When you use negative labels you run the risk of the child believing the label and beginning to act that way. Instead, describe specifically what behavior you think is "mean" or "rude." Below are two vague problems and several possible specific behaviors for each problem.

Vague problem definition	Possible specific definitions
1. My 12 month old is rude.	a. He grabs my glasses.
	b. He won't wave goodbye to grandma.
	c. He sticks his tongue out at the neighbor.
2. My 2½ year old is lazy.	a. She wants me to find her doll all the time.
	b. She wants to be carried all the time.
	c. She won't clean up her room when I tell her to.

For each of these problems, there are many more possible specific problem behaviors, but not all of them will be seen as problem behavior by any one person. It is often hard to force oneself to decide *specifically* what behavior is unacceptable, but when you have done so the problem usually becomes much, much more manageable.

Exercise 2-1: Problem Definition

TWO: Gather data

When a child's behavior reaches the stage that it is considered a problem, the parent often feels as though the behavior occurs all the time. Thus it is helpful to gather some data. Three useful pieces of information are the actual frequency of the problem, the context of the problem, and the developmental level of the child or children involved. We will look at each of these ideas briefly.

The frequency with which a behavior occurs is obtained simply by setting aside a specific period of time (minutes, hours, or days) that you will watch the child and record the number of times the behavior occurs during that period. It is often more accurate to average several observations rather than to use just one. The record is useful for two reasons: (1) it gives the parents an objective look at how often the behavior occurs, and (2) it provides a baseline against which the parent can measure change. For example, a record of frequency of rudeness for the child in situation 1 (on the previous page) might show that the child really grabbed his mother's glasses only once a day. If the mother makes some change in how she handles her child, but the result is that he grabs her glasses three or four times a day, she will know that she is increasing the problem rather than decreasing it. Thus a record of frequency of the specific behavior may be helpful in evaluating the solution.

Observing the context of the unacceptable behavior is also helpful. The context might include when and where the behavior occurs and who else is involved. Understanding the context of the problem often gives a parent a clue as to how to handle the situation. For example, biting often occurs for one of two reasons: (1) the child is teething and likes the feel of biting, or (2) the child uses biting as a means of getting what he wants. In the first case, something else can be substituted; in the second, the child needs to learn more appropriate means of getting his way or expressing anger.

Check the developmental level for the behavior you want the child to perform. What is possible and what is typical for children changes dramatically during the first four years. It is important to remember also that before each skill is perfected, there is a long period of unsuccessful attempts. A one year old who uses a spoon without spilling much is very unusual; however, by two years, most children can use a spoon. Likewise, most children can remove their clothing by 24 months, but less than one quarter can put on simple clothing at that age. It is not until four years of age that three quarters of the children can dress themselves without supervision. An understanding of child development might have helped the parents cope with some of the problem behaviors described previously. For instance:

Exercise 2-1: Problem Definition

INSTRUCTIONS: Look at the statements below and write a specific behavioral statement of the problem to replace the vague statement.

A. Matthew (2½ years old) is a cry baby. When I leave him, he cries and clings to me making a big fuss. He is the biggest baby around.

_____

_____

B. Mary (3 years old) is a lazy dawdler. She won't concentrate on dressing unless I am right there beside her. If I leave, she begins to look at a book, play, or whatever. I have trouble getting her ready and getting to work by 9 AM.

_____

_____

C. Margaret (18 months old) is so uncoordinated, she can't do anything. She can't even build a tower of four blocks like Amy. Whenever Margaret tries to build a tower, the blocks fall down and she whines and cries.

_____

_____

POSSIBLE ANSWERS: **A.** *Matt cries when I leave him.* **B.** *Mary needs my company to dress.* **C.** *Margaret can't build a tower of four blocks.*

__Example 1a.__ Most babies are intensely curious. They will often reach for glasses, mustaches, or beards on a face, especially if they are not familiar with them. If curiosity and intellectual development are traits you value, then you will need to respond to the problem in a way that does not destroy curiosity.

__Example 2a.__ Around two, most children can obey simple specific commands or requests. (For example, four or five word commands like "Please bring me the book" or "Put your doll there, please.") When there is a large mess, it is difficult for the toddler to decide which toy to pick up and where to put it.

The child's cooperation in the cleaning task can be encouraged, however, by delegating to her small parts of the solution. For example, say, "Put the trucks in this box." This way the child needs only to decide which trucks to start with.

Exercise 2-2: Developmental Levels

Exercise 2-2: Developmental Levels

INSTRUCTIONS: *Look up the age at which most children (75%) develop the ability desired by the parent in the preceding exercise (2-1). The developmental chart is on page 12.*

A. Matthew — separates easily from his mother.

_____

B. Mary — dresses without supervision.

_____

C. Margaret — builds a tower of four blocks.

_____

ANSWERS: **Matthew:** *75% of children separate easily at age 3½.* **Mary:** *75% of the children dress without supervision at 4 years.* **Margaret:** *75% of children can build a tower of four blocks at 20½ months.*

Determine who owns the problem. Dr. Thomas Gordon, in his material on Parent Effectiveness Training, explains the concept of *problem ownership.* Problem ownership divides behavior in three groups depending upon "whose needs are not being met." Let us look at how this works in three situations.

Child owns the problem. My two-year-old daughter is playing with a dump truck in her room and is crying because she can't make it work. She is in her room with the door closed so that, although I am aware she is upset, I am not being disturbed. The child owns the problem because her needs are not being met. My needs are not being interfered with in a tangible way.

No problem. Next, my daughter has the truck working well and is driving it around. She takes a load of blocks from her room and dumps them on the living room floor. She enjoys the dump truck and I enjoy watching her. There is no problem in the relationship because my child's needs and my needs are being met.

Parent owns the problem. Finally, my daughter tires of driving the blocks around and goes outside and gets a load of sand. She dumps the sand on the living room rug. I don't like sand on the rug. I own this problem. My child's needs are being met, but her behavior has interfered with my needs in a tangible way.

The placement of a specific behavior into one of these categories will vary from person to person. For example, when Mark rides his scooter in the living room, his "mother owns the problem" because the furniture is new and she is afraid he will scratch it. Riding a scooter in his Aunt Mary's house is "no problem." The furniture there is old and the room is large. In yet another home, it could become the child's problem if the room was too small to permit the scooter to move easily. Look at the situations in Exercise 2-3 and decide "who owns the problem."

Exercise 2-3: Problem Ownership

The choice of solution depends on who owns the problem. When the child owns the problem, the most effective technique to deal with the problem, particularly if you value independence and responsibility, is active listening. Active listening (discussed in Chapter 3) offers the child support, but permits the child to retain control and responsibility for his own problem. If the parent owns the problem, there are three alternatives open. First, you can modify yourself. This can be done by reviewing your values, developmental expectations, and your needs to see if you can redefine the behavior as acceptable. The second alternative is to alter the environment (discussed in Chapter 6) to increase the probability of a more acceptable behavior occurring. The third alternative is to alter the child's behavior. This can be done by explaining your needs and feelings using I-messages (in Chapter 3) or other techniques presented in Chapters 3, 4, and 5.

THREE: Generate potential solutions

Generating solutions can be done formally or informally. In either case, however, the goal is to get as many alternatives as possible. I have found that the first four or five solutions generated are usually ones the parent has already been toying with, and that the most creative ideas usually come after they have been cleared out of the way.

Separate the generation of ideas from their evaluation. Some people limit themselves by rejecting ideas immediately because they "know" they won't work, they are too time consuming, or they are too expensive. There are many things you can do in every situation. Sometimes an idea that is not good or practical itself will spark a really good idea.

It is often easier to think of alternatives in terms of needs rather than in terms of solutions. For example, if your 14 month old takes the books off the book shelf, a *solution* would be to spank him when he touches a book. The *need*, however, would be to have your books remain unmolested. When you think in terms of needs, you could — move your books up higher, put a barrier in front of your books, teach the child to handle books carefully, get your child his own books to explore, etc. Each of these can be implemented in several ways providing even more alternatives.

Pick a problem you have, determine your needs, and see if you can come up with many alternatives. Some of them may be pretty farfetched, but that is fine.

Exercise 2-4: Generating Solutions

Exercise 2-3: Problem Ownership

INSTRUCTIONS: Look at the situations below (from Exercise 2-1) and decide "who owns the problem" and what needs are not being met.

A. **A parent with a crying child**: "Matthew (age 2½) is a crybaby. When I leave him, he cries and clings to me making a big fuss. He is the biggest crybaby around."

Who owns the problem? _____

What needs are not being met? _____

B. **Parent with a slow dressing child**: "Mary (age 4) is a lazy dawdler. She won't concentrate on dressing unless I am right there beside her. I have trouble getting her ready and getting to work by 9 AM."

Who owns the problem? _____

What needs are not being met? _____

C. **Parent with a frustrated child**: "Margaret (18 months) is so uncoordinated, she can't do anything. She can't even build a tower of four blocks like Amy. Whenever the blocks fall down, she whines and cries."

Who owns the problem? _____

What needs are not being met? _____

POSSIBLE ANSWERS: These are possible answers. Your answers will vary depending on how you see the needs of the parent and the needs of the child.
A. *Matt owns the problem — he needs his mother's reassuring presence. OR*
    The parent owns the problem — she is bothered by the noise.
B. *Mary owns the problem — she needs a lot of time to dress.   OR*
    The parent owns the problem — s/he needs to leave on time.
C. *Margaret owns the problem — she cannot do what she is trying to do. OR*
    The parent owns the problem — s/he does not want to hear Margaret whining and crying.

**FOUR:
Evaluate,
choose and
implement
an idea**

Now is the time to cross ideas off the list that are too expensive, too time consuming, too damaging to the child's self-esteem, in conflict with your values, or whatever. Ideally, the solution chosen should meet the needs of everyone involved — both parents and children.

Items rejected because they are "too time consuming" or "won't work" may need to be further examined. Often ideas that are initially time consuming may save time later. For example, teaching your child to put on his clothes may be time consuming, but it could save you fifteen minutes a day or over 90 hours a year. Some ideas are branded "won't work" by parents who assume that the child's point of view is the same as the adult's. For example, I have

Without Spanking or Spoiling

Exercise 2-4: Generating Solutions

INSTRUCTIONS: Choose one of the situations below (from Exercise 2-1), look at the unmet needs and generate several solutions.

A. "Matthew (age 2½) is a crybaby. When I leave him, he cries and clings to me, making a big fuss. He is the biggest baby around."

B. "Mary (age 3) is a lazy dawdler. She won't concentrate on dressing unless I am right there beside her. I have trouble getting her dressed and getting to work by 9 AM."

C. "Margaret (18 months) is so uncoordinated, she can't do anything. She can't even build a tower of four blocks like Amy. Whenever the blocks fall down, she whines and cries."

Problem: _____

_____

Unmet needs: _____

Possible solutions:

1. _____
2. _____
3. _____
4. _____
5. _____
6. _____
7. _____
8. _____
9. _____

POSSIBLE ANSWERS: These are possible answers for Mary the slow dresser. Your answers will vary with the situation you chose and your assessment of it. **Problem:** Mary dresses slowly alone. **Needs:** Father needs to be on time to work.
Possible solutions: (Reminder — When generating solutions, do not limit yourself to acceptable ones.)

1. Father could schedule work later and get up at the same time.
2. Get Mary up earlier, so she would have more time.
3. Take Mary to the babysitter's in her pajamas.
4. Read Mary a story if she is dressed on time by herself.
5. Dress Mary yourself.
6. Give Mary a treat for breakfast if she is ready on time.
7. Let Mary wear her clothes to bed.
8. Have Mary dress in parent's room while the parent dresses.
9. Have Mary dress in the kitchen while breakfast is being fixed.
10 Have Mary dress at the neighbor's.

seen several children happily accept a cookie broken in half when they asked for two, although the mother insisted it wouldn't work. Many small children simply want a cookie for each hand, and if they don't see it being broken, are content with one part for each hand.

Many problems arise in child management because parents start by implementing a solution without defining the problem, checking their expectations, or generating solutions. They assume that either there are no alternatives or that they know best.

FIVE: Evaluate your solution

It is important to evaluate the solution. If it is successful, then pat yourself on the back; if not, then try again. You will know very soon if the solution you chose works, because the unacceptable behavior will stop or decrease. If the solution does not work, go back to step one and begin the process again. If it does work, make notes and try the method again on a different problem. After you have had several successes, it is nice to look back on the problems you no longer have.

Try putting the problem solving process together on a problem you have. The steps are briefly outlined in Exercise 2-5.

Exercise 2-5: Review a Problem

Additional reading

P.E.T.: *Parent Effectiveness Training* by Thomas Gordon. Peter H. Wyden, New York, 1970.
□ Chapter 13: Putting the no-lose method to work.

Exercise 2-5: Review a Problem

INSTRUCTIONS: Pick a problem that has been bothering you and follow it through the steps below.

1. Define the problem behaviorally.

_____

2. Gather data:

    A. How frequently does the behavior occur? _____

    B. When is the behavior most likely to occur (place, time, or people involved)?

    _____

    C. Is the problem common at your child's age? _____

    D. Problem ownership: Who owns the problem? _____

              What are the unmet needs? _____

3. List alternatives:

_____

_____

_____

_____

_____

4. Evaluate & choose. Evaluate the alternatives. Which alternative is best for everyone? Develop a plan.

_____

_____

5. Revise. If the problem persists, which alternative will you choose next?

_____

How did it go? (Evaluate your solution)

_____

Chapter 3: Avoiding Problems

Many of the problems and frustrations for parents can be avoided by clear, honest communication and by planning. This is as true when the child is a baby as when the child is a preschooler. There are four general rules to follow to reduce the frequency and intensity of conflicts: (1) give adequate forethought to what you are doing or will be doing; (2) make your expectations clear; (3) clarify all feelings involved; and (4) follow through with your decisions.

Adequate forethought

Adequate forethought is developed by learning from experience. With all children, infant through teens, there are some times or activities that will cause frustration for all involved. With some children, it is whiny times or reluctance to go to bed; with others, it is refusal to share toys or inconvenient demands for attention. When you can predict what times or situations will be difficult, you can plan to meet your needs and your child's needs too. This may involve planning activities to reduce boredom, restructuring time, planning transitions, or foreshadowing events. Each of these possibilities will be discussed below.

Reduce boredom. When children are bored, they are often whiny or demanding. Boredom in children arises from either the lack of appropriate activities for the child's developmental level, or the inability of the child to seek out activities to occupy himself. The way to resolve boredom depends on the cause. If, for example, the child becomes bored while you are travelling in the car or visiting a childless friend, then the solution is relatively easy. Plan to take toys or activities that the child enjoys. In some cases, it may be well to have some special "traveling" toys that the child likes but may use only when he or she is visiting. Planning activities for children works for short trips, such as grocery shopping, as well as for long distance trips.

There are many books available now that offer ideas for activities or toys for children. Most books are available in the public library and in book stores. You may want to borrow a couple of the books from the library first to see which ones you like, and then purchase the one(s) you like best to have on hand.

If the child is bored because he cannot seek out activities on his own when they are available, the problem is more complex. Some parents unknowingly encourage this situation by creating or permitting dependence on themselves or on television. When activities are continually provided, watching television is encouraged, or the child is frequently interrupted during play, the child does *not learn* to seek out activities on his own. If the boredom is mild, the easiest solution might be to provide one or two appropriate activities (but not more, because it is more difficult to choose among them) and let the child play uninterrupted. It is important also to keep in mind the child's basic temperament and developmental level so that your expectations are reasonable. If your child paints a nice picture or builds a tall block tower, consider well before you interrupt her with your praise. If your greatest concern is encouraging artwork, praise her. However, if you are more concerned with increasing her attention span, skip the praise. If your child asks for your appreciation, then it is fine to give it; but do not *interrupt* the child to do so. Sometimes the habit of interrupting a child is so compelling that the parent needs to leave the room to avoid disturbing the child.

If the child's boredom is causing much frustration, a more active solution may be needed. The most effective technique would probably be to use shaping (in Chapter 5), but that is a time consuming method. Providing activities for a child who cannot seek out her own will solve the short-run problem (what to do now) but will not reduce the long-run problem (inability to occupy oneself).

Exercise 3-1: Interaction Log

Restructure time. Research has shown that most children are more frequently frustrated in the late morning and late afternoon. This has been associated with hunger, tiredness, and illness. If your child becomes "difficult" at the same time each day, then you may wish to rearrange the family schedule to eliminate or reduce the fussy period. Schedules can be rearranged in many ways: changing meal times; providing snacks; changing sleeping or nap times; instituting a quiet time; omitting, rescheduling, or reducing house cleaning; cooking simpler meals and freezing them; etc. The following are two accounts of how time can be restructured to make the day more pleasant.

In our family, the hour and a half from 4:00 to 5:30 PM (when my husband arrives home from work) was very unpleasant. I tried to fix dinner while both my children were hungry, tired, and wanted my attention. I made three changes that improved the situation greatly:

(1) I changed my toddler's nap time so she slept later in the afternoon and was less tired in the evening. She was a little more cranky at noon, but I was less frustrated by it.

(2) I gave my children a substantial snack when my son got home from school.

(3) I prepared several meals at the same time and froze the extras. This was usually done in the morning or in the afternoon while my toddler napped. In the evening, I could put the dinner in the oven and was then free to respond to my children or read the newspaper.

Karen (16 months) was usually a sweet child. However, when she got overtired, she was difficult to deal with. These difficulties became acute when she and her mother began to attend a toddler-mother class that was over at her nap time. By the time they got home, prepared and ate lunch, and got diapers changed, Karen was too tired to take her nap.

Exercise 3-1: Interaction Log

INSTRUCTIONS: *Select two periods (about 30 min. each) to record the frequency and type of interaction you have with your child. The periods may be on the same or different day, but they should be at different times during the day.*

Record the number and types of interactions with your child, and who initiates them (parent or child). An interaction may be for instruction, attention, discipline, or whatever.

NOTE: *This exercise will be most objective if someone else records their observations of you and your child, but it is still very useful if you do it yourself.*

First Period: Day _____, Time _____, Setting _____

Second period: Day _____, Time _____, Setting _____

Her mother solved this by changing Karen's diaper before they left class, and feeding her a sandwich and fruit slices in the car on the trip home. By the time they got home, Karen was ready to go to bed.

When you are looking for ways to restructure time, determine what the underlying needs for you and your family are, and then generate as many ways as possible to meet these needs.

Exercise 3-2: Difficult Times

Plan transitions. Transitions (such as bed time, meal times, departures) often cause frustration between toddler and parent. The frustration arises in part from the child's need for independence and in part from her inability to predict what happens next. This can be seen in the example below.

Cathy (27 months) loved to take baths. After she had enough splashing, she would hop out and ask to be dried. When she was dry, she would usually return to the tub and play in the water again. To avoid having to dry her two

Exercise 3-2: Difficult Times

INSTRUCTIONS: *Review the last couple of days and your interaction log (Exercise 3-1) and then answer the questions below.*

1. What time of day are *you* usually most frustrated?

2. What time of day is *your child* most frustrated?

3. What activities are most frustrating for you when they are interrupted?

4. What activities is your child most likely to have difficulties or frustration with?

5. How can you restructure time or activities to reduce some of these frustrations?

(1) _____

_____

(2) _____

_____

(3) _____

_____

or three times, her parents would let the water drain from the tub before drying her.

Transitions can be made more smooth by making your expectations clear, letting the preceding activity fade out naturally, and providing rituals. If you make the habit of thinking ahead to what will happen next, you may occasionally realize that starting a certain activity should be postponed because your child is too absorbed to be stopped willingly or too active to make a smooth transition. A story or quiet activity will often help a child calm down and change gears for meals or bed.

A ritual, or particular way of doing things, also helps. It signals to the child that soon dinner, bed time, or whatever will soon be here. An evening ritual might consist of pajamas, quiet play, story, and then bed. Some rituals include a snack, others a bath. What is most important is that it be something that your child likes and you can live with.

Foreshadow. Foreshadowing involves preparing a child for an experience or event that is new or uncomfortable. Children are often afraid of the unknown, and display inappropriate behavior in new situations because they do not know what is appropriate. Foreshadowing involves explaining (1) what activities will take place, (2) what the child will be expected or permitted to do, and (3) what she may feel like. Foreshadowing is particularly useful with a child whose initial response to new situations is withdrawal.

When the child is less than two, explanations need to be short and concrete. Since it is difficult to convey an idea or experience that is new to a preverbal child, a "dry run" is often helpful. When the child is over two, you can begin to explain things through stories and role playing. We can see how foreshadowing works in the example below.

When Tammy was 2½, she was very uncomfortable in new situations. She was invited to a birthday party and her mother felt she needed to prepare Tammy for the event.

Her mother reviewed what happens at a birthday party. She decided that the following items were important: (1) activities — Tammy would take a present; there would be several other children; they would sing Happy Birthday, eat birthday cake, and play some games. (2) Tammy would be expected to enter into these activities except, perhaps, for the games. Finally, (3) she might feel shy, insecure, or jealous.

Mother explained this to Tammy first by recalling a party she had gone to as a child, then by acting out the story with dolls. Her mother got a record with Happy Birthday on it from the library, and she and Tammy sang it and other songs. Next they had a pretend party for one of Tammy's dolls, complete with presents, cake and ice cream, and a game. The preparation took a lot of time, but it was useful for Tammy since she was able to attend the party without being uncomfortable.

There are many situations that can be foreshadowed: trips to the doctor, dentist, or museum; arrival of a sibling; trips to grandparents or the seashore; attending an adult meeting — basically anything that has been difficult or that experience suggests might be difficult. *Mr. Rogers* has several picture books that deal with some of these topics, and there are many more books in most libraries. A caution: read a book completely to yourself before reading it to your child. If you have any concerns or negative feelings, don't use the book.

Make your expectations clear

Small children see the world from a dramatically different perspective than adults. The difference arises both from their small size and their limited experience. The English language is full of "polite commands" — questions that are really not questions, but rather orders; and questions that offer choices that do not really exist. For example, "Do you want to wash up for dinner?" or "Would you like to go home now?" These non-questions are terribly confusing to young children.

Speak at the child's level. When you wish to enlist a child's cooperation, it is important to speak at his or her level. This means both getting down to the child's eye level, and using language the child can understand.

It is most uncomfortable for a child to maintain eye contact with an adult who is standing next to him. The child must tilt his head back in an awkward position and hold it there during the conversation. If you have ever been caught seated on the floor and participated in a conversation with someone standing above you, you may recall the feeling of discomfort. Most good preschool teachers understand the discomfort of looking up, and kneel down or bend over while talking to a child. In addition to the discomfort, looking up makes most people feel intimidated. Again, if you wish to gain the child's cooperation, it is best to get down to his level.

When preschoolers begin to speak in six or seven word sentences, parents often assume that the children can understand most of what is being said. The parents are right, but the word "most" is a bigger catch than they realize. Preschoolers are very literal and interpret adult requests and actions in the light of their experience, which is limited. The difference between the child's and adult's perspectives can be seen in the examples below.

Kitty's mother was seated on the floor sorting clothes. Kitty (27 months) asked her mom to read a story. Her mother said she would when she was finished sorting the laundry. Kitty started to chant: "Do-it-now, do-it-now, ..." Her mother responded to the chant by saying, "Stop, hold on a minute." At this, Kitty immediately stopped chanting and grabbed her mother's arm. (Kitty thought she was doing what her mother told her to do.)

One evening, Kevin (age 4) and his mother went for a walk after dark. Just for the fun of it, she asked him how many moons the earth had. Without hesitation, Kevin replied, "Two." She asked him to explain and he said, "We have one circle one and one line (crescent) one." (Kevin's experience clearly indicated two moons.)

*Beth (2½) and her mother were eating lunch and there was not much soup left in the pan. Mother asked Beth if she would like a little bit more soup. Beth replied, "No, I wan-na **big** bit more. I a big girl."*

A parent can check a child's understanding by asking the child to explain what he (the parent) has said or what will happen in a given situation. Let the child explain in his or her own words. Note that asking the child "Do you understand me?" will not be helpful because most children will respond "Yes" because they think they understand, or think their parents want them to say "Yes."

Questions vs. commands. It is common to hear a parent say to his or her child, "Would you like to go the store now?" or "Do you want to go to bed?" Most adults recognize these as the commands, "Now is the time to go to the store" and "It is bed time." Young children, however, take the questions literally, and will probably answer, "No." To avoid confusing the child, make your expectations clear. Give an order if you want him to do something. Ask a "yes" or "no" question only if you are willing to accept either answer.

Once you have asked the question and your child says "No," the best procedure is to respond, "Okay, we will go in five minutes. I will set the timer so you will know." Then, when the timer rings, rephrase the sentence to, "Now it is time to go to the store," or bed, or whatever.

Limited choice vs. free choice. When you give your child a free choice, he may come up with anything. When you give your child a limited choice, you restrict his or her alternatives to choices that are acceptable to you. If, for example, you offer the *free choice*, "What do you want for breakfast?", the alternatives are unlimited. The answer could be cereal, or eggs, or pizza, or ice cream, etc. If you offer a *limited choice* in the decision ("Do you want eggs or cereal for breakfast?"), you have restricted the possible answers to foods you are willing to prepare. If you are only willing to accept a limited number of possible alternatives, offer a limited choice rather than a free choice.

Guided choice. Sometimes when you offer a child a limited choice, they refuse both options. If that happens, you can then offer a guided choice. For example, if you ask your toddler, "Do you want to put on your red jamies or your blue jamies?" and she says, "No!", you can rephrase your question to offer the guided choice: "Do you want to choose or do you want me to choose?" If she says "No" again, you can say, "I see you want me to select your pajamas tonight."

You can find ideas for the guided choice by considering what you would do if the child refuses your request. For example, few children wish to go to bed. If you ask, "Do you want to go to bed?" the answer will most likely be "No!" Instead ask, "Do you want to walk to bed or be carried to bed?" Most of the time children will opt for the face-saving approach. If they don't, you can reply, "I see you choose to be carried to bed."

Grandma's rule. Grandma's rule is a technique for clarifying what you expect to happen. For example, "*When* you put your blocks back, *then* we will read a story." It is important to note that this is *not a choice*. The child was not offered, "*If* you put your blocks away, *then* we will read a story." The if-then structure implies a choice, and the child may choose not to have a story and to leave the blocks on the floor when she is done. The when-then structure implies an expectation. The child is expected to perform the first act, and then the second will follow.

Exercise 3-3: Making Expectations Clear

Clarifying feelings

Some problems can be avoided if parents are aware of their own feelings and those of their children. Strong feelings, such as fear, frustration, or impotence, often paralyze our creativity and problem solving abilities. When parents take the time to sort out their feelings toward unacceptable situations, new solutions become possible. When a child is having a problem, the parent can reflect the child's thoughts and feelings. This reflection makes it easier for the child to think of new solutions.

Exercise 3-3: Making Expectations Clear

INSTRUCTIONS: Rephrase the sentences below in the command that is implied or in a choice you are willing to accept.

1. Janey, it is cold. Do you want to put your sweater on?

   _____

   _____

2. Do you want to help me pick up the toys, Mark?

   _____

   _____

3. Peter, what do you want for breakfast this morning?

   _____

   _____

4. Mary, do you want to put away your clothes before we go to the park?

   _____

   _____

5. Ann, why don't you let me help you get dressed now?

   _____

   _____

6. Terry, what do you want to wear to Sunday School this morning?

   _____

   _____

7. If you finish your liver, we can go for a walk.

   _____

   _____

8. Brannon, do you want to put that glass ash tray down?

   _____

   _____

*POSSIBLE ANSWERS: **1.** Janey, put your sweater on. OR Janey, do you want to wear your blue or yellow sweater? **2.** Mark, help me pick up the toys. OR Mark, which toys do you want to pick up? **3.** Peter, do you want your eggs scrambled or fried? **4.** Mary, when you put your clothes away, we will go to the park. **5.** Ann, I will help you get dressed now. **6.** Terry, do you want to wear your blue outfit or your red outfit to Sunday School today? **7.** When you finish your liver, we will go for a walk. **8.** Brannon, put the glass ash tray down.*

Becoming aware of feelings. Children respond differently when their needs are not met. A child may cry, whine, pout, bite, chew his nails, or withdraw. Children vary naturally in the intensity of their responses (see Exercise 1-5, page 16). Many children are taught to hide their feelings. However, because a child does not respond intensely on the outside does not mean that he or she does not feel strongly on the inside. A study found that boys who were calm, cooperative, and restrained internalized their anger and other emotions more than the less inhibited boys. It is incorrect to assume that because a child does not *act* angry that he or she is not angry. Children and adults both need to recognize their feelings and learn to deal with them constructively. Several children's books which discuss feelings and ways to deal with them are included in the readings at the end of this chapter.

Exercise 3-4: Recognizing Feelings

Active listening. Active listening is most effective when the child owns the problem. When a child has a problem, active listening can be used by the parent to help the child solve the problem himself. Active listening with the verbal child involves reflecting both the content and the feelings of the child's message. When a parent active listens, she is concerned but not involved — no questions are asked, no solutions are offered. The child is encouraged to clarify the problem for himself or herself, and to find his or her own solutions. If the child asks for assistance, it may be provided, but assistance should not be volunteered. Once the problem is clarified in the child's mind, the solution often becomes clear also. Let's see how this works in the situation below.

Karl, who was accustomed to fixing his own cereal, came storming into the bathroom where his mother was occupied.

Karl:	*"Mommy, there is no milk!"*
Mother:	*"You feel frustrated because there is no milk."*
Karl:	*"Yeah, go get some right now!"*
Mother:	*"I will go when I am finished in here."*
Karl:	*"I want it NOW!"*
Mother:	*"You are very frustrated because you want breakfast now and there is no milk and you don't know what to do."*
Karl:	*"Maybe I could make some powdered milk."*

One of the great advantages of active listening is that it promotes problem solving by the child rather than a dependence on adults to solve problems. Active listening promotes long-term problem solving rather than a short-term solution. It takes more time and patience to active listen with a child than to solve his problem yourself or to "guide" him to the solution, but active listening will save time in the long run. The child will learn how to think for himself, rather than to turn to adults for guidance and support.

Parents ask: "Well, aren't there times when I have to ask questions to find out what happened?" or "Aren't there times when I have to solve the problem for my child?" The answers to both are, "yes." Particularly with preschoolers, there are times that you will want to know what happened or provide insight that they have not had the chance to gain. But toddlers and

Exercise 3-4: Recognizing Feelings

INSTRUCTIONS: Think about times when your child is hurt, worried, or frustrated.

A. How does your child respond?

____ cries	____ bites	____ slams the door
____ sucks thumb	____ retreats to room	____ bites nails
____ whines	____ stomps feet	____ pulls hair
____ cuddles blanket	____ withdraws in self	____ holds breath
____ hits	____ runs	____ other: _____
____ sulks	____ becomes quiet	____ other: _____

B. Are your child's methods of expressing frustration, and other feelings, acceptable?

____ Yes ____ No: if not, how would you like your child to express his or her feelings?

_____

_____

_____

_____

preschoolers are capable of solving many more problems than they are given credit for because parents *assume* they are too young and offer help before they have a chance to try several solutions. I had the chance to relearn this myself when my daughter was little.

Karen (19 months) and I were at her toddler class. We were in the gym where a lot of climbing equipment was available. My daughter saw a two and a half year old climb into a suspended mesh tube. She went over and tried to climb in too. She was unable to balance on one foot and maneuver the other foot into the tube. After a few minutes she gave up. My inclination was to help her or show her how to get something to climb on to get in, but I didn't.

A few minutes later she came back and tried again, still with no success. She came over to me with a long face. I resisted the temptation to help her and said, "You're disappointed that you can't climb in the tube," to which she nodded and wandered off.

A little while later, she came back again and tried. This time she threw the upper portion of her body into the mesh tunnel and then pulled both her legs in after. She succeeded in getting in herself! I was so glad I did not assist her, because she learned a valuable lesson — that she can solve her own problems. If I had put her in, I would have had to do it many more times;

if I had shown her a solution (i.e., moved a chair over), she would never have found her own.

If Karen had asked for my help, I would willingly have given it to her, but she did not. To provide unasked-for assistance implies that the other person is not capable of finding a solution on her own. Many times parents offer solutions before children have a chance to think of their own. Active listening can be particularly useful for parents who value independence, intelligence, and competence for their children. Parents usually offer solutions because they don't want their child to be frustrated or unhappy. However, by regularly providing solutions for children, parents actually increase the probability that their children will be frustrated when their parents are *not* around to solve their problems.

Active listening can also be used when the child's feelings are more intense than the example above. In the illustration below, the father begins by explaining things to his daughter, and when that did not work, tries active listening.

Kathy, aged 2½, was upset when her mother refused to let her play with a new, expensive watch. She cried for several minutes. Then her father tried to calm her down by asking her to tell him what was wrong. She replied, "I wanna Mommy watch." At this point Father explained to her that it was a new watch and Mommy wanted to wear it herself. After this Kathy began to cry again and continued to demand the watch.

One or two minutes later, her father tried again, telling her that she was crying so much that he could not understand what she said. She stopped crying and replied, "I wanna Mommy watch." And he replied, "You wish you could play with Mommy's watch." After that she just looked at him for a little bit, and then began to play.

Parents of preverbal toddlers and babies often think that their child is "too young" to understand what is said, so they don't bother with active listening. While it is true that preverbal children cannot understand *precisely* what is said, they understand the general meaning of things long before they talk well. Even young infants pick up feelings of fear, frustration or relaxation in the atmosphere around them. Before the child is mobile, the parent will need to "solve the baby's problems" because the baby is physically unable to help himself. If the parent accompanies his actions with active listening — "You feel really hungry, you want something to eat" — the baby will learn two things: first, that the adult's voice means comfort is coming and she can begin to relax; and second, that there are words to describe how she feels without needing to cry.

Toddlers are learning labels for the things and actions around them. Even toddlers that are not talking are learning the meaning of words. When a parent talks about how the child feels or how he himself feels, the child learns the words the same way he learns other descriptive words (like "hot," "fast," "nice"). This can be seen in the examples below.

Amy (16 months) was playing with a pull toy underneath the table. The string got caught around the table leg. Amy pulled on the string and cried loudly. Daddy came over and said, "Your toy is caught. That frustrates you. Would you like me to untangle it for you?" Amy nodded.

Sam (13 months) was standing quietly at the window watching his mother leave. His father, noticing his long face, said, "You're disappointed that you cannot go with your mother today." Sam said nothing and looked out the window again.

It is unlikely that Sam or Amy knew what the words "disappointed" or "frustrated" meant. However, they did get a sense of parental concern and some information to begin building a feeling vocabulary with. Often parents wait to use feeling words until they think their child is old enough to understand them, forgetting that children need a long period of introduction before they can develop concepts for them.

Exercise 3-5: Active Listening

I-messages. I-messages are used to clarify a problem when the parent owns the problem. I-messages are also useful for modeling a constructive way of handling anger or an unpleasant situation. The most common format for the I-message is: "When ..., I feel ... because ... ." The *when portion* is a specific non-blameful description of the child's behavior. For example, "when a child interrupts me" is more specific than "when a child is rude" which describes a personality trait. The *I feel portion* expresses your primary feelings about the behavior or the results of the behavior on you (mad and angry feelings are not usually primary feelings, but follow some other feeling such as helplessness, fear, or injustice). The *because portion* states the tangible effect of the child's specific behavior on you — particularly time or money involved. The three parts do not have to be used in the same order and other wording can be substituted for the "when," "I feel," and "because." Several examples are presented below.

*"**When** people scribble on the wall, **I feel** frustrated **because** I will have to clean it off."*

"When you climb on the banisters, I am afraid you will fall and get hurt."

"Loud noises near my ears upset me because they hurt my ears."

"I get discouraged when the room I just cleaned is messed up before I get a chance to enjoy it, because I have no time to do what I want to do."

Strange as it seems, small children may not know *why* something bothers their parents. They may be able to predict that their behavior will bother them, but they can see things only from their point of view. I-messages will usually work unless the child has a strong need of his or her own to continue in that behavior, or if the child does not believe that his behavior really affects you. When the child continues, you must follow your I-message with another skill from the following chapters.

Exercise 3-6: I-messages

Exercise 3-5: Active Listening

INSTRUCTIONS: Look at the situations below and determine what clues the child gives that he or she is having a problem, and what feelings he or she may be feeling.

1. Steven, 2½, is sitting on the sofa with a thumb in his mouth staring at Alan playing with some Preschool Legos on the floor.

    Behavioral clue(s) _____

    Possible feelings _____

    Active listening response _____

    _____

2. You hear a loud thump from the living room followed by a wail. You find Ricky (12 mo.) lying on the floor in front of the sofa crying.

    Behavioral clue(s) _____

    Possible feelings _____

    Active listening response _____

    _____

3. Christy is sitting in front of a shape sorting box, loudly banging a square peg on the triangular hole.

    Behavioral clue(s) _____

    Possible feelings _____

    Active listening response _____

    _____

POSSIBLE ANSWERS:

1. *Behavioral clue: thumb in mouth.*
Possible feelings: rejected, ignored, bored
Possible response: "You feel lonely in here."

2. *Behavioral clue: loud cry*
Possible feelings: hurt, frustrated, scared
*Possible response: "You hurt yourself on the floor." **or** "You are frustrated that you can't climb on the sofa."*

3. *Behavioral clue: loud banging*
Possible feelings: frustration
Possible response: "You can't get that block in the hole and that frustrates you."

Grant in fantasy. Granting in fantasy what you cannot grant in real life is another way to acknowledge feelings. You do this by discussing the request as though you could grant it. For example:

We had been on the road since early morning and four-year-old Nicholas was getting tired of riding. He saw a familiar fast food sign and demanded we

Exercise 3-6: I-messages

INSTRUCTIONS: Rephrase the statements below to form "I-messages."

1. Don't play on the stairs, you'll fall!

_____

_____

2. (Parent, trying to read a newspaper): Quit bothering me!

_____

_____

3. If I've told you once, I've told you a thousand times, close the front door!

_____

_____

4. Get this stuff picked up off the floor or you won't get any dessert tonight.

_____

_____

5. If you hit your sister again, I'll beat the tar out of you!

_____

_____

*POSSIBLE ANSWERS.   NOTE: These are only possible answers. Your answers may vary depending on the consequences of the behavior **to you** and **your feelings** about it.*
1. *When I see you playing on the stairs, I am afraid you will fall and hurt yourself.*
2. *When the sofa bounces a lot, I get frustrated because I can't read the newspaper.*
3. *When the front door is left open, the flies come in and I have to stop fixing dinner to kill them, and that annoys me.*
4. *I get discouraged when I see the room I just cleaned up all messy, because I will have to do it again when I would rather read.*
5. *When someone hits your sister, I am afraid it will hurt her.*

Without Spanking or Spoiling

stop and get an ice cream cone. As I drove I explained that it was not lunch time yet, and that we still had awhile to go before we could stop. Nicholas was not impressed. He began to chant, "Ice Cream, ice cream," and kick the back of my seat.

Before I exploded, Mike, his dad, turned and said "I am the magic cone man. Nicholas, would you prefer chocolate or vanilla?"

"Vanilla," Nicholas replied.

"How big a cone would you like? This tall or bigger?" Mike asked motioning with his hands.

"Bigger! This big," Nicholas answered as he spread his hands nine inches.

Mike and Nicholas went on to discuss the type of cone, possible toppings, and the best ways to lick a cone. The mood in the car changed dramatically from confrontational to cooperative. I wouldn't have believed it if I had not seen it.

Follow through with your decisions

The small child usually judges what you will do more from what you have done in the past than from what you say you will do this time. This again reflects their dependence on personal experience for explaining their world. For this reason, it is wise to avoid repeating the same request or command, to think about what you "threaten" or promise before you speak, and to assist your child in complying with your commands.

Avoid repeating yourself. Burton White, in his book *The First Three Years of Life*, states that parents of "competent children" did not repeat their requests. If the child did not comply after the first time, they would get up and help the child do what was requested. For example, suppose a father told his son to get off the table and his son remained on the table. The father would go over to the child and "help" him climb down from the table, rather than remain seated and repeatedly order the child to get down. By assisting the child to comply, the child learns what the parent really expects him to do. Repeating commands teaches a child that the parent only expects compliance after the second or third request.

Think before you speak. If you really want your child to believe you, it is simplest to offer only choices or consequences that you are willing and able to provide. This means that you don't threaten to throw away all toys left on the floor or promise a treat when you get home unless you will do precisely what you said. Often this means you must stop and think when you get angry to avoid saying something that you will regret or back down on.

If you find you have said something that you cannot carry through (and all parents do sometimes), it is best to tell the child why you have changed your mind rather than simply not carry through your threat. Changing your mind won't matter much if it happens a couple of times; however, if you find yourself frequently in a situation in which you do not carry through, it would be wise to review those types of situations and see if they can be avoided (see Adequate Forethought, page 33).

Set the stage for compliance. Since young children learn from what happens to them, it is sometimes helpful to arrange things so the only thing or the easiest thing for the child to do is what the parents want. This is illustrated in the example below.

Two-year-old Beth liked to throw kindling on the fire (which her parents permitted). However, when the time came to stop, it was often difficult for her to resist, especially with the kindling box sitting beside the fireplace. Her father would tell her to put one last piece on the fire and then he would remove the box, so it was easy for her to resist the temptation.

In this situation, it was easy for Beth to avoid throwing wood on the fire because the kindling was not there to tempt her. There are many ways to modify the environment to make it easier for the child to do what the parent wishes. (See Modifying the Environment, Chapter 6.)

Assist compliance. Assisted compliance involves physically intervening to help a child comply with your request. Compliance is necessary, for if you tell your child to do something and you do not follow through, you teach your child to ignore you. For example, if you say, "It's time to go now," you must leave and resist the temptation to be sidetracked or delayed. If the child does not come willingly, ask "Do you want to walk or be carried?" If he doesn't start for the door, pick him up and carry him out.

When children are still small, you can help them comply. Once children learn that you will follow through, there will be much less testing. The number of times it will take to learn, however, depends upon the child's temperament. Some children are challenging even when you are consistent. These are the children that most need your gentle persistence.

With most children it is easier to avoid problems than to deal with the behaviors when they arise. In this chapter we have looked at using adequate forethought, making your expectations clear, clarifying feelings and following through with your decisions. In Chapter 4 we will look at ways to encourage desirable behavior.

Additional reading for avoiding problems

Parent Effectiveness Training, by Thomas Gordon. Peter H. Wyden, Inc., Publ., New York, 1970.
  □ Chapters 2, 3, and 4: Active listening
  □ Chapters 5 and 6: I-messages
  □ Chapter 8: Modifying the environment
How to Talk so Kids will Listen and Listen so Kids will Talk, by Adele Faber and Elaine Mazlish. Avon Books, New York, 1982.
  □ Chapter 1: Helping children deal with their feelings.
Love and Anger, The Parental Dilemma by Nancy Samalin with Catherine Whitney. Penguin Books, New York, 1991.
Talk about Feelings series: *Nathan's Day* (1991) and *Ellie's Day* (1989), by Susan Levine Friedman and Susan Conlin. Parenting Press, Inc., Seattle, Washington.
Dealing With Feelings series: *I'm Mad, I'm Frustrated* and *I'm Proud*, by Elizabeth Crary. Parenting Press, Inc., Seattle, Washington, 1992.

Chapter 4: Increasing Appropriate Behavior

The key to improving your toddler or preschooler's behavior is reinforcing his or her appropriate behavior. The young child is learning a lot about *both* what behavior is appropriate (how to get attention) and how people interact (what type of attention is available). Your child will develop a preference for the types of attention (praise, spanking, scolding, smiles, etc.) you give her, and will soon find out what needs to be done to get more (i.e., patting her sister, pushing her sister, coloring on the floor, putting "wet" in the toilet). If your child can get your attention and praise by putting her toys away, then she is more likely to continue doing so. If the only way she can get your attention is to hit her sister, then she is likely to continue to hit her.

Two concepts are mentioned above that we will look into further: the concept of attention (or strokes in transactional analysis) and the concept of reinforcement (in learning theory). Transactional analysis and learning theory are both general theories of why people behave as they do. First we will look at attention, and then we will look at positive reinforcement and praise.

Attention

We all have certain basic needs. One of our basic needs is for stimulation or recognition from outside ourselves. This recognition often takes the form of attention. Early studies indicated that when babies were not stimulated (held or stroked), they failed to grow and develop well. The need for interaction (or attention) begins at birth and lasts until death.

Attention can be positive or negative, that is, pleasant (a smile) or unpleasant (a scolding). Attention is so essential that if a person cannot get a positive message, he or she will provoke negative attention. There is an old saying that "if a child can't get a kiss, he'll take a kick."

Negative messages differ from I-messages (page 44) or logical consequences (page 82) in that the negative message is usually a negative statement *about the child*, rather than about the child's behavior. I-messages clarify how the child's *behavior* affects the parent, and consequences clarify possible results of the child's behavior for the child.

People become accustomed to the type of messages or attention they get. If children are ignored when they ask for positive attention, but get responded to (or scolded) when they do something "bad," they may learn to prefer negative messages. The strong desire for attention is illustrated in the example below.

Two-year-old Cindy brought a book to her mother and tried to climb on her lap. Her mother brushed her off, saying "Later, Cindy." A few minutes later Cindy returned with the book. Again her mother brushed her off, saying

"Later, I am reading now." This time Cindy went to the book shelf and started throwing the knick-knacks on the floor. Her mother stopped immediately and scolded Cindy at length for throwing things on the floor. In the example, Cindy wanted her mother's attention enough that she chose a scolding rather than being ignored.

Messages can be conditional or unconditional. A conditional message says "I like (or dislike) you when you do certain things." An unconditional message says "I like (or dislike) you because you are you." Four general kinds of messages are possible: conditional positive messages, unconditional positive messages, conditional negative messages, and unconditional negative messages. Examples of these four types of attention are presented below.

Four Types of Messages

	Unconditional	Conditional
Positive messages	I love you.	I like your behavior when you play quietly.
	You're a nice person.	Mommy will be pleased with you if you play gently with the baby.
Negative messages	I hate you.	Mommy will be angry at you if you hit the baby again.
	You're a pest.	No jumping on the sofa.

Unconditional positive messages build a child's self-esteem. Conditional positive messages help build acceptable behavior. Children need both conditional and unconditional positive messages. Children who receive only unconditional positive messages may develop to be selfish and unruly. Children who hear only conditional positive messages may be well-mannered and cooperative, but feel unsure and unloved.

Exercise 4-1: Recognizing Types of Attention

Attention takes many forms. We have talked so far primarily about verbal attention. However attention can be physical like a hug or a spanking, facial like a smile or frown, or paying attention like watching or listening. Most young children have a strong need for physical attention. When they no longer need to be carried, they may look for excuses to be held — like being read stories or being rocked.

Attention preferences vary, both for the same person and between people. As a person, I need different attention (or types of interaction) at different times. When I have just finished making a child's toy, I want it admired. When I have an interesting idea, I want to talk about it. When I feel affectionate, I

Exercise 4-I: Recognizing Types of Attention

INSTRUCTIONS: *Before each situation below, indicate if the attention given was positive (+) or negative (-), and if it was conditional (c) or unconditional (u).*

+/- or c/u

_____ _____ 1.   To girl in a new dress: "Wow, you look nice in that dress."

_____ _____ 2.   Response to child who has requested help: "What do you want now, dummy?"

_____ _____ 3.   To child approaching the TV set: "If you touch the TV knobs again, I won't like you any more."

_____ _____ 4.   To child while you are taking a walk: "I like you."

_____ _____ 5.   To child hanging up his coat: "That's nice."

_____ _____ 6.   To child who has just broken the large vase: "You're a bad boy. A bad, bad boy."

_____ _____ 7.   To child in bed: "Good night and sweet dreams."

_____ _____ 8.   To child about to pour milk on the floor: "Mommy will be mad at you if you dump your milk on the floor."

_____ _____ 9.   To child who has dumped all the toys (blocks, books, and puzzles) on the floor and won't help clean them up: "You're so much trouble, I wish you weren't born."

_____ _____ 10. To child who climbs on Daddy's lap with a book: "I'm glad you're my boy."

_____ _____ 11. To child approaching a younger baby: "If you hit him again, I will know you're a bad boy."

_____ _____ 12. To child struggling with clothes: "I'm glad you are putting your pants on by yourself."

ANSWERS:

1. +c	3. -c	5. +c	7. +u	9. -u	11. -c
2. -u	4. +u	6. -u	8. -c	10. +u	12. +c

want to be cuddled. However, cuddling when I want to be listened to is annoying; and praise when I want to be cuddled is wasted. Some children want active involvement (by rocking or reading) and other children want to be watched or have someone nearby while they play. When an adult tries to hug a child who doesn't want a hug, the child will squirm in an attempt to get free; however, the same child may be delighted by your sitting near or being watched while she plays.

Attention preferences vary between children. There are some children who would be content to sit on someone's lap for a long, long time; and there are other children who do not like to be on a lap unless they are hurt or sick. These differences between children are often apparent from infancy.

Asking for attention is okay. Much of the time, people do not know what form of attention other people want, so it is important to be able to ask for what you want. The value of attention is not diminished because it is asked for. The hug you give a baby when she raises her arms to be held is as valid as the one you initiate. Unfortunately, as the child begins to move around on her own, adults often cease to respond to the child's requests for positive attention. At that time, the child learns new ways to get positive messages, or switches to negative messages which are more predictable.

A critical question for parents to answer is: "How do I want my child to ask for attention?" Put another way, it's "How do I want to be interrupted?" It is not realistic to say "I don't want to be interrupted," because that ignores the child's basic needs. As in the example with Cindy (page 49), the child will get through somehow. First Cindy tried for a story, and when that failed, she tried a method she knew her mother would not ignore. The parent has the choice of how she is reached.

Exercise 4-2: Attention Preferences

Focus time

One way parents can satisfy their child's need for attention is to set aside a specific time each day to spend with that child alone. The time can be spent with either the father or the mother, but should be regular enough for the child to count on. To be most effective, the time needs to be centered on the child's wants or needs. Focus time should not be structured by the parent, but by the child. For example, focus time is not the time to teach letters, numbers, etc., unless the child initiates it. Sometimes the child may simply want the adult to sit nearby and watch him (caution: time spent daydreaming, answering the phone, or sneaking a peek at a book is not focus time.) Interestingly enough, many parents have found that devoting as little as fifteen minutes a day to a child noticeably reduces the demands and disruptive behavior at other times.

Positive reinforcement

Learning theory or behavioral modification is usually very effective in changing the behavior of toddlers and young preschoolers, *but* it is less effective at fostering problem solving on the part of the child, so it is best used with other methods.

The basic premise of learning theory is that people *learn* to act the way they do. Someone or something has taught each of us to behave the way we do. Old behaviors can be unlearned and new behavior learned to take their place. Learning theory has four concepts which are involved in changing the behavior of young children: positive reinforcement, reinforcement schedules, ignoring, and negative reinforcement. The first two topics will be covered in this chapter, and the last two will be covered in Chapter 6.

Positive reinforcement increases positive behavior. Positive reinforcement is accomplished by using a positive reinforcer — something that increases the frequency of the behavior that immediately precedes it. A positive reinforcer can be anything that a child wants or needs. It can be food, praise, attention, toys, or whatever the child desires. The effect of a positive reinforcer is lost or

Exercise 4-2: Attention Preferences

INSTRUCTIONS: Read the situations below and answer the questions regarding attention preferences.

1. You have just finished painting a room and replacing all the furniture.

    a. How would you like your spouse to react when seeing the room for the first time?

    ____ compliments   ____ thanks   ____ other: _____
    ____ a kiss or hug   ____ smile

    b. If your spouse did not come into the room (and therefore has not seen what you did), how would you handle the situation?

    _____

    _____

    c. How would you like your spouse to ask for recognition if the situation were reversed?

    _____

    _____

2. You have really had a rough day. Your spouse was gone, so you took the kids to the zoo and then out to eat. Nothing went right. Everyone seemed to give you trouble.

    a. When your spouse returns that evening, what would you like him or her to do?

    _____

    _____

    b. If the situations were reversed, what would you like your spouse to do?

    _____

    _____

dramatically diminished by even short delays between the behavior and the reinforcement.

With positive reinforcement, as with other child guidance techniques, the parents need to decide exactly what they want (specific behavioral definition), determine whether the behavior is reasonable for the child's age (check developmental level), and check the frequency of the desired behavior. Let us see how positive reinforcement works with a simple example.

Alice (age 2½) occasionally (once a week) puts her dirty clothes in the laundry hamper when she takes them off. Her father would like her to put them in the hamper regularly. The laundry hamper is in Alice's room and easy for her to use. Her father decides to positively reinforce "putting dirty clothes in the laundry hamper" with praise.

Since the desired behavior is one that Alice does occasionally, her father waited until she put her clothes in the hamper next. When that happened, he immediately said, "Alice, I am really pleased that you put your clothes in the hamper." The next night when she remembered again, he promptly reinforced her with, "Wow, you remembered to put your clothes in the laundry hamper again tonight. I'm really pleased."

The next evening, however, Alice forgot. Her father said nothing and put the clothes in the hamper himself. The next several nights Alice remembered to put her clothes in the hamper and was positively reinforced each time with praise.

In the example, Alice's father defined the desired behavior specifically, checked her developmental readiness, chose a potential reinforcer, and reinforced the behavior promptly each time it occurred.

Positive reinforcement can work for you, as it did for Alice's father, or it can work against you if you are not aware of what is going on. Positive reinforcement is more likely to work against you when the positive reinforcer is something that appears unpleasant to adults like spanking or scolding. Let us look at two more situations and see what is being learned in them.

1. *Toddler hangs up his coat on a hook for the first time. Mother notices immediately and says, "I'm proud that you hung your coat up." He smiles at her, then goes to play. The next day, the child hangs up his coat again.*

2. *Father is busy paying the family bills. His daughter tries to get his attention and is ignored. She then removes all the cushions from the sofa and begins to bounce on them. Father stops working and yells at her to put the cushions back. She slowly puts them back on the sofa.*

In both cases the parent's attention was a positive reinforcer for the child's behavior. In the first situation, the child is learning to hang his coat up; in the second, the girl is learning to get her daddy's attention by jumping on the cushions. It often surprises parents that spanking and yelling can act as positive reinforcers and increase the very behavior they are intended to discourage. The reverse can also be true, that you will do something nice and expect it to act as a positive reinforcer, but it does not. It may have no affect at all or it may act as a negative reinforcer and decrease the desired behavior. If you think you are reinforcing a behavior, but the behavior does not increase, then the reinforcer is not working. Some possible reasons are discussed on page 58.

What to reinforce. There are two general ways to use positive reinforcement. First, and most obvious, is to reinforce the behavior that you like. The behavior can be specific (like dressing or putting toys away), or general (like personality traits that you value). For example, if a parent valued obedience, she might want to reinforce her child occasionally for doing what she asks immediately. Or, if someone valued self-control, he might wish to reinforce a child's self-restraint, particularly in a situation that he knew was difficult for the child. You may wish to check the children's traits you value (Exercise 1-2, page 10) and recall what particular behaviors were important to you. The second way to use positive reinforcement is to reinforce an acceptable substitute for an unacceptable behavior. Some guidelines for selection of a substitute behavior are discussed in Chapter 6.

Double learning. In each child-parent interaction, there are two sets of learning going on: first, what the child is learning; and second, what the parent is learning. Let us look back at the two examples above and see what the parent learned. In the first situation, the mother was learning to praise her son to get what she wanted. She praised him, he smiled, and then repeated the desired behavior the next day. In the second situation, the father was learning to get what he wanted by giving his daughter attention (in this case, yelling). He yelled at her and she began to put the cushions back. In each situation, both parent and child are learning.

Exercise 4-3: Identifying Reinforcers

Reactions to positive reinforcement. "Why should I reward my child when he does what he is supposed to do?" The primary reason, as I mentioned above, is to encourage your child to continue that behavior. When you positively reinforce a behavior, your child knows you like that behavior and is more likely to continue than if you did not reinforce it. For example, you are more likely to wear and feel good in a shirt you have received several compliments on than one you have not been complimented on.

"But I don't want to reinforce my children all the time for everything they do that I like!" Fortunately you don't have to. We will discuss when and how to reduce positive reinforcement in the section titled "Reinforcement schedules affect behavior retention" (page 57).

"Positive reinforcement sounds an awful lot to me like bribery. Is there really a difference?" YES! One way to look at it is that there are short-term rewards, long-term rewards, and intermediate rewards. A short-term reward is a bribe. A bribe is used to *stop* the negative behavior that precedes it. A bribe or short-term reward reinforces an undesirable behavior. You must continue to use a bribe to get the same results. A bribe stops the "undesirable" behavior temporarily, but it does not increase the desirable behavior.

A long-term reward immediately follows a desirable behavior and strengthens the desirable behavior rather than an undesirable behavior. In the purest form, a long-term reward arrives unannounced. An intermediate reward lies between the two. To clarify the difference, let us look at the situation below:

Yesterday Mother drove several children to the park. On the way, her son Arthur began to poke his friend. Arthur was requested to stop, but continued. The situation got worse until everyone was upset and unhappy.

Exercise 4-3: Identifying Reinforcers

INSTRUCTIONS: *In each of the situations below, a behavior is being reinforced. Decide what behavior is being reinforced and what the reinforcer is.*

1. Mary (1 year) falls down, looks up at her mother, and then begins to cry. Mary's mother rushes over and comforts Mary.

   behavior reinforced: _____

   positive reinforcer: _____

2. Annie (2½ years) is building a castle, Peter (9 mo.) crawls over and knocks it down. Annie asks her mother to "make Peter go away." Mother continues to read her book. Peter knocks the blocks down again, and Annie pushes him away forcefully. Mother hears Peter cry and comes rushing over to scold Annie and take Peter away.

   behavior reinforced: _____

   positive reinforcer: _____

3. Ricky (18 mo.) spills some water, looks at the mess a bit, and then gets a sponge and smears it around. Mother smiles and says, "I'm glad you are wiping up the water you spilled."

   behavior reinforced: _____

   positive reinforcer: _____

4. Karen (15 mo.) runs to the door in the evening when her father comes home saying, "Hi, dada! Hi, dada!" He picks her up and says pleasantly, "Hi, punkin, how's my girl today?"

   behavior reinforced: _____

   positive reinforcer: _____

5. Matt (24 mo.) brings a book to his father and asks for it to be read to him. Dad ignores him and continues to read the newspaper. Matt then goes and takes a toy away from his baby brother causing him to cry. Dad stops reading and scolds, "Give that toy back this instant! Bad boy! Bad, bad boy!"

   behavior reinforced: _____

   positive reinforcer: _____

ANSWERS:
1. *Mary was reinforced for crying by attention and comforting.*
2. *Annie was reinforced for making Peter cry by removal of Peter.*
3. *Ricky was reinforced for wiping up the spilled water by praise and attention.*
4. *Karen was reinforced for greeting her father by attention.*
5. *Matt was reinforced for taking a toy away from his brother by scolding and attention.*

Today Mother is worried about whether there will be trouble again, and she has brought some granola bars to use as a reward.

Short-term reward: *Mother waits until the trouble starts, then says that the children may each have a granola bar if they calm down. They immediately calm down and she gives them a granola bar.*

Long-term reward: *Mother keeps the bars a secret at first. Then, before the children cause trouble she hands them out, saying she is glad that they have been calm and pleasant in the car.*

Intermediate reward: *Mother announces, as the children get in the car, that she has some granola bars for them if they are pleasant and calm until the timer rings. The children are calm and Mother gives them each a bar when the timer rings.*

In the first case, the children learned the way to get a snack is to have a fit. In the second and third cases, the children learned to get a snack by being quiet. In the first case, the parent will always have to "pay" for the quiet. In the second and third cases, the reinforcement can be gradually reduced.

Reinforcement schedules affect behavior retention. Positive reinforcement would become burdensome if you had to reinforce a child every time for every thing she did that you liked. Fortunately, that is not the case — the reinforcement schedule can be varied. The reinforcement schedule is the relationship between the number of times a behavior occurs and the number of times it is reinforced. When an activity is reinforced every time it occurs, learning is quickest; but when the same behavior is no longer reinforced, forgetting is also quickest. A new behavior that is intermittently reinforced is much more slowly learned, but also more slowly forgotten when no longer reinforced. The easiest way to speed learning *and* encourage retention is to positively reinforce the behavior each time it occurs *until* it is learned, and then to reduce the frequency of reinforcement until you positively reinforce the behavior only once a month or so.

Reducing the frequency of reinforcement should be done with a definite plan rather than by whim. The first time you skip reinforcing a behavior, it is often helpful to appear involved in something else rather than simply refusing to reinforce the behavior. It is particularly important to see that the child gets reinforced the next time he performs the same behavior so that unlearning does not begin. Let us look again at the example of Alice and see how her father reduced the frequency of reinforcement.

After Alice put her dirty clothes in the hamper regularly, her father decided to change the reinforcement schedule. The next evening when Alice took her clothes off and put them in the laundry hamper, her father appeared to be putting away some of her toys. While he put them away, he peeked to see how she reacted to the lack of reinforcement. She seemed a little disappointed, but continued putting her pajamas on.

The next evening when she put her clothes in the clothes hamper, he told her, "Boy, you sure remember to put your clothes in the hamper well. You remember even when I am busy with something else and can't watch you."

During the next week, her father reinforced her four times, three times a week during the following two weeks, and occasionally, once or twice a week, after that.

Positive reinforcers can be anything that your child wants, needs, or would like to have. It can be time, attention, candy, food, money, tokens, stars, anything. When you offer something as a reward, you are saying that this is special and good. If you use one type of reward to the exclusion of others, you can increase its importance to the child. For example, if food or candy is frequently used as a reward, it can encourage the use of food as comfort. Likewise, if you frequently use story reading as a reward, reading may become very important. One catch is that the item or activity *must* be perceived as desirable to the child or it will not work.

The most powerful positive reinforcer for most toddlers is the parents' time and attention. Parents or childcare providers are the toddler's primary source of attention since he does not have strong peer friendships yet. Attention can be given in the form of praise, a gesture, or a shared activity. The use and misuse of praise is discussed in the next section of this chapter. A shared activity can be used as a reward immediately ("I'm so pleased with the way you put your blocks away, let's go for a walk") or by presenting a ticket for the activity to a preschooler. The use of a ticket with older preschoolers is useful for situations where you cannot enter into the activity immediately. When you use tickets, there must be an understanding about when they may be redeemed. This agreement should be rigidly adhered to by the parents or the tickets will lose all value. It is important to remember that to be a positive reinforcer, the activity must be desired by the child. No matter how attractive the intended reinforcer is to the parent, if it is not wanted by the child, then it is not a positive reinforcer.

Reinforcers can lose their effectiveness. Reinforcers, even very strong ones, can lose their effectiveness. This happens when the child becomes satiated or "full" of the reinforcer. For example, an ice cream cone might work well to reinforce a behavior that occurred once a day. However, if the child received four or five ice cream cones a day, it would not be many days before an ice cream cone's motivational power would decrease. A child can become satiated with almost anything — gold stars, trips to the park, M&Ms, or praise. If you have a behavior that is taking a long time to establish, you may need to change reinforcers a couple of times.

Common problems using positive reinforcement. If you are trying to reinforce a behavior, but the behavior is not increasing, something is wrong. There are four questions to consider in clarifying the problem.

(1) *Am I positively reinforcing the behavior **immediately** after the behavior takes place?* With small children, a delay can destroy the usefulness of positive reinforcers for the desired behavior.

(2) *Am I positively reinforcing the desired behavior every time it occurs?* Learning takes place faster when the child is rewarded *every* time the

behavior occurs. (Note: when the behavior is established, change the reinforcement schedule.)

(3) *Is the "reward" something that the **child** really wants?* Occasionally parents offer something they expect the child to like, but the child is indifferent to or actually dislikes the potential reinforcer.

(4) *Is the desired behavior specific enough that someone else could observe it and reinforce your child?* Sometimes parents know the general behavior desired, but cannot clearly explain it to others. If another adult cannot clearly discriminate the desired behavior, it is probable that the child cannot either.

Praise

Praise is one of the most common forms of positive reinforcement. It has the advantage of always being available. Like most guidance tools, however, it can be used either effectively or ineffectively. Effective praise tells the child "I like what you did," immediately follows the desirable behavior, and is sincere.

Effective praise is specific. Specific praise states what the child did and how you feel about it. For example, "Tommy, I am pleased that you hung up your coat." You can praise a task completed or the effort of trying. If you were to say only "Good boy," Tommy would be less sure whether you were pleased with him in general, for hanging up his coat, for closing the front door, for the thought in his head, or something entirely different. Specific praise reduces the possibility of misinterpretation. General praise, such as "nice job," or "good work," are somewhat less ambiguous when the child is obviously trying to do something and finally succeeds. General praise often contributes to a feeling of well-being and competence, but it can backfire if the child himself does not feel "good" or "nice" at the moment. When that happens the child may do something to show the parent that he or she is not nice or good after all. This would have been avoided if the parent had said what he saw or what she felt about the situation, because what was being praised would be clear.

Praise must immediately follow the desired behavior. If there is a delay using praise, even for a short time, praise will lose its effectiveness for promoting the desired behavior. This means that if you want to reinforce your children's playing cooperatively, you must remain nearby so that you can praise them immediately, rather than having to come back into the room to praise them. (Note that it is often best to praise them just before they break up, rather than to interrupt while they are playing well, otherwise they may not continue to play well after you have praised them.)

Praise must be sincere. Children always know when praise is not sincere. If you are not pleased with how things turned out in general, but you wish to praise the child, find a part that you are pleased with and praise that portion only. For example, if your daughter brings you a picture that she drew that does nothing for you, don't say "That's nice, Mary." Find something about the picture that you like (the colors used, an interesting shape, the way the whole paper was colored, how hard the child worked on it), and praise that part.

Ineffective praise. The surest way to lose the value of praise is to couple it with a negative comment or comparison. This is sometimes called the sandwich approach to praise. For example, "Terry, I am glad you put your toys away today; I hope you won't forget tomorrow." The negative reference to tomorrow's expectations takes the pleasure out of the praise. It leaves the child with the feeling that she is not doing very well. Sometimes parents, particularly of older children, try to reduce the sting of a complaint by sandwiching it between praise or compliments. The message children get is that the situation is too undesirable or dangerous for honesty.

A child can also become satiated with praise. Positive comments are important for the development of positive self-image, but if the frequency or intensity is too great, they can lose some effectiveness as motivators. This sometimes happens when a parent is trying to potty train a child and is so happy when the child has finally urinated in the toilet that she overwhelms the child with praise.

Exercise 4-4: Recognizing Effective Praise

In this chapter, we have looked at ways to increase positive behavior through recognizing the need for attention, reinforcing desired behavior, and using constructive praise. These are the most potent tools you have for changing behavior. They can be used to help teach new skills and to erode negative behavior. They are effective because they tell the child what he may do, not what to avoid. Some books are listed below for those wishing to do additional reading in this area.

Additional reading

Improving Your Child's Behavior by Madaline C. Hunter and Paul Carlson. Bowmar Press, Glendale, California, 1971.
  □ Chapter 2, Positive Reinforcement
  □ Chapter 5, How to Reinforce

T.A. for Tots by Alvyn M. Freed. Jalmar Press, Sacramento, California, New Edition, 1991.

Win the Whining War and Other Skirmishes, by Cynthia Whitham, MSW. Perspective Publishing, Los Angeles, California, 1991.

How to Talk so Kids will Listen and Listen so Kids will Talk, by Adele Faber and Elaine Mazlish. Avon Books, New York, 1982.
  □ Chapter 5: Praise

The Incredible Years: A Trouble-Shooting Guide for Parents of Children Aged 3-8, by Carolyn Webster-Stratton, Ph.D. Umbrella Press, Toronto, 1992.
  □ Chapter 2: Praise
  □ Chapter 3: Tangible Rewards

Exercise 4-4: Recognizing Effective Praise

INSTRUCTIONS: *Place an "E" by examples of effective praise and an "I" by examples of ineffective praise.*

For ineffective praise, indicate what is wrong and how you would change it to effective praise.

_____ 1. I'm glad you remembered to bring your blanket to Grandma's. That was good thinking.

_____ 2. I'm glad you remembered to go potty. I hope you won't forget next time.

_____ 3. For such a little boy, you did very well.

_____ 4. The room looks really nice. You put your blocks away, the puzzle away, and the books away.

_____ 5. (To a small child trying to get his pants on, but not managing) Boy, you sure gave those pants a workout. Putting your clothes on is hard. I'm glad you tried to dress yourself this morning.

_____ 6. Well, now you look like a human being without the oatmeal in your hair.

_____ 7. I see you are sharing your big blocks with Ricky. That's nice. I'll bet he was happy to play with them.

_____ 8. It was so nice when you played quietly before lunch. Could you play quietly now?

_____ 9. (To child who has come in after putting his trike away) Good job!

_____ 10. (To child who has brought in a long slimy worm that disgusts his parent) Yes, Suzy, it is a pretty worm.

ANSWERS

1. Effective, specific.
2. Ineffective. Negative comparison: *I hope you won't forget next time.*
   Change: *I'm glad you remembered to go potty.*
3. Ineffective. Negative comparison: *"Such a little boy"* implies that the job was not really satisfactory.
   Change: *Nice job!*
4. Effective, specific.
5. Effective, specific (for trying, not for success).
6. Ineffective. Negative comparison: *You didn't really look human (good) before.*
   Change: *You really look clean.*

7. Effective, specific.
8. Ineffective (if it is the first mention after lunch). Delayed: *The children should have been praised before lunch.*
   Change: *You kids really have been playing quietly.*
9. Effective, general. (Praise specific behavior, not general)
10. Ineffective. Dishonest: the parent did NOT feel the worm was pretty.
    Change: *My, that worm really is long.*

Chapter 5: Teaching New Behaviors

Encouraging positive behavior is great if the child occasionally does what you want, but sometimes there are things you want a child to do that he has never done before. There are three techniques you can use to teach a young child something that he does not already do: modeling, simple instruction, and shaping. These techniques will be presented in this chapter after we consider several factors that influence the effectiveness of teaching new behaviors.

Factors affecting learning

The emotional climate. Learning takes place *only* when no problems exist. Long-term learning rarely takes place when the parent (teacher) or the child (student) is upset. It is important, therefore, to stop the "lessons" before the child or parent becomes upset or tires of the activity.

The child's developmental level. Learning cannot take place unless the child is developmentally ready. It is fruitless to spend large amounts of time trying to train a child to do something that she or he is simply not ready for. For example, you can spend seven months teaching a six-month-old child to walk or wait until he is a year old and dramatically reduce the time and hassle. The same is true for toilet training. The process will be much shorter if the parent waits until the child can hold urine, urinate at will, and recognize a full bladder in time to reach the potty.

In addition to physical readiness, adults also need to be aware of the child's ability to understand concepts. To illustrate this, let us look at what is involved in learning colors. It is relatively easy for children to memorize the colors of common objects like a traffic light (red light) or a pair of shoes (blue shoes) as a part of their names. To really understand color, however, the child needs to identify the attribute of an object that is called "color." To do that, he needs to understand "same" and "different," and to develop a concept of each hue. (When, for example, does red stop being red and become purple, or orange, or pink?) Until the child has formed these concepts, attempts to teach him color are bound to cause frustration to all concerned.

The style of learning. Children learn especially well through concrete experiences rather than from instruction. For example, children get a better understanding of "full" and "empty" from playing with cups in the sand box or bath tub than from watching an illustrated episode on *Sesame Street*.

The child's expectations of himself or herself. A child who expects to learn will learn more quickly than one who expects difficulty. The following situation illustrates how this can work.

One mother had tried unsuccessfully to toilet train her child several times. Finally she told her son that when boys are three (four months away), they put their urine in the potty and wear big boy pants. They then checked with several three-year-old and older boys to see that it was true. The day he was three, he wanted to know where his big boy pants were because he was going to put his urine in the potty. This time the training went very smoothly, unlike previous attempts.

If the parent can plant the expectation that the child will make a change (learn a new behavior) after a particular time (for example, after a holiday, a birthday, or grandma's visit), it often makes the learning process easier.

These factors affect the ability and willingness of the child to learn. Teaching attempts that disregard these factors are usually time consuming and disappointing.

We now present three methods of teaching new behavior: modeling, simple instruction, and shaping. These methods can be used alone or in combination.

Modeling

Modeling is perhaps the most powerful way of teaching behavior. Toddlers are natural mimics. They will try to do almost everything they see adults and other children do. They attempt to read books, set the table, dress in their parents' clothes, and use tools just as they have seen their parents do. This intense modeling can be used to advantage.

If you wish to teach a skill or behavior by modeling, you must do *exactly* what you want your child to do. If you would like your child to pick up the toys, then do so in the child's presence; if you want your son to cook, then do so in his presence; if you want your daughter to use a new toy, then play with it in her presence. Picking up the toys or cooking alone is not enough, it must be done in the child's presence. Otherwise the child may conclude that it just happens as the sun rises and night falls without intervention. Once the desired behavior occurs, positively reinforce it in some way, or it may fade out. Many parents assume that if a child begins a behavior, he will continue it. This is not true unless the behavior or skill is enjoyable for the child himself.

It is wise to remember that children may model anything they see or hear. They will pick up some of your "desirable" and your "undesirable" traits. If you want your children to speak quietly, then you should speak quietly. If you do not want your children to smoke, then you should not smoke. As children grow older, they begin to model what they see outside their family and what they see on television. For example, one woman spent a lot of time convincing her son not to cram cookies into his mouth like Cookie Monster does.

Exercise 5-1: Recognizing Modeling

Simple instruction

Simple instruction, both verbal and with gestures, can be used to teach a child a new behavior. When toddlers are given instructions, both the instruction (verbal or with gestures) *and* the concept conveyed must be *very simple*. Very simple instructions with gestures can be used before the toddler can speak,

Exercise 5-1: Recognizing Modeling

INSTRUCTIONS: Modeling begins very early. It involves speech patterns and gestures as well as behavior. Look at your child's actions and answer the three questions below.

1. List several things your child already does that imitate you or other persons in your family.

    _____

    _____

    _____

    _____

    _____

2. List two habits or traits you or your spouse have that you hope your child **will** pick up.

    _____

    _____

3. List two habits or traits of yours or your spouse that you hope your child **will not** pick up.

    _____

    _____

because the ability to understand speech precedes the ability to speak. However very young children cannot remember more than one command at a time. Ideally, verbal instructions should be less than five words long. When the statements are accompanied with gestures, the expected behavior should become clear. This is illustrated in the following example.

Mom wished to teach nine-month-old Paul to climb off the furniture backwards. When Paul crawled near the edge of the sofa, she would turn him around saying "turn around" and then gently pulled his feet off, saying "feet first." After several repetitions, Paul began to turn around by himself and slide off feet first.

Exercise 5-2: Using Simple Instruction

Shaping   Some activities are so complicated or so difficult for toddlers that they cannot learn the whole skill or make the complete change at one time. Shaping is a technique that breaks a larger task or goal into smaller, more manageable

Exercise 5-2: Using Simple Instruction

INSTRUCTIONS: Read the situations below and decide what verbal instructions and what gestures you would use to teach the child the skill involved.

Situation A: You are sitting on the floor with your daughter and a ball. You would like to "teach" her to play ball.

Your instructions: _____

_____

Your gestures: _____

_____

Situation B: You are trying to put your son's jacket on him. His arms are either straight down or wiggling all around.

Your instructions: _____

_____

Your gestures: _____

_____

Situation C: Your 20-month-old son would like to help sort the dirty clothes.

Your instructions: _____

_____

Your gestures: _____

_____

POSSIBLE ANSWERS:

Situation A: Say, "Push the ball," while making a pushing motion.

Situation B: Say, "Stand like this," while holding his arms out horizontally. Follow with similar instructions when other positions are needed.

Situation C: Say, "Socks here, pants here," and point first to the dark pile, then to the light pile.

pieces. Shaping can be used to teach a new skill or improve one that exists.

The technique of shaping requires some advance planning and observation. There are four general steps: assessing the situation, developing a plan, implementing the plan, and evaluating and revising the plan.

Assess the situation. If you wish to use shaping to improve a current skill, like independent play, you need to determine the current frequency or level of the skill. You can do this by requesting the child play alone and timing the length of play on each of three or four days. If the skill is completely new, check whether it is appropriate for the current age level of the child, and whether the child has shown any interest in the activity.

Develop a plan. The plan should include breaking the skill down into small steps, deciding how you will explain these to the child (i.e., modeling or simple instruction), and how you will reinforce the learning of each step. When you have divided the process into steps, you can have the child either start with the first step and work towards the end, or start with the last step and gradually add steps on toward the beginning. If you are teaching a completely new skill, you will probably need to reinforce attempts to take the steps as well as actual success with each step.

Implementation. When your plan is complete, and both parents and child are in the "no-problem" — i.e., neither is upset — time, you may begin shaping. Since learning only occurs in the no-problem time, you will stop or active listen (page 41) with the child if he becomes frustrated. Initially, reward the child for success with each step. When he has completed the first step successfully several times, gradually increase the complexity of the task (by adding more steps) or increase the length of activity needed to receive reinforcement.

Evaluation and revision. It is important to evaluate your progress after two or three times so you do not waste a lot of time and create unnecessary frustration should the learning not go as you planned. If you are progressing, then continue with your plan. If you are not progressing, then see if (1) the problem can be broken into even smaller steps, (2) the child knows what is expected of him, and (3) the child is really ready to learn.

Let us look at how shaping would work with a relatively simple example. Mother wants Tanya (age 20 months) to put her dirty clothes in the clothes basket. In this situation, the child has not previously shown the desired behavior.

Putting clothes in the laundry hamper is a skill that Tanya has not exhibited; however, her mother feels that she is capable of learning since she can walk well alone and has been throwing all sorts of other things into the laundry basket.

Mother plans to divide the task into three parts:

1. picking up the dirty clothes,
2. taking them to the laundry basket, and
3. throwing them in.

Mother decides to start with Step 3 and work backwards towards Step 1. She will use both modeling and simple instruction to teach the behavior, and she will use praise and a hug as reinforcement.

After Tanya is in her pajamas, Mother picks up Tanya's clothes and takes her over to the laundry basket. As Mother throws the socks in, she says, "Put it in." Next she gives Tanya her shirt and tells her, "Put it in." When Tanya looks puzzled, Mother tosses in the undershirt, again saying, "Put it in." When Tanya puts the shirt in the basket, Mother gives her a hug and says, "You did it!"

The next evening, Mother throws in one article and Tanya puts in the remaining ones. Mother begins to work backward from there.

By the fourth day, Tanya puts all her clothes in the laundry basket as they are handed to her. At the end of a week, Tanya will pick them up and put them in the laundry basket herself.

Shaping can also be used on a more complex task, where it is more difficult to explain. Let us look at how shaping would work where Janet's parents would like her to play alone longer.

Once each on Monday, Tuesday, and Wednesday, Janet's mother asked her to play by herself a while. The length of the sessions were 2, 4, and 3 minutes.

Mother and Father decided that it would be reasonable for Janet to play alone for 10 minutes. They will reinforce independent play with attention before she quits. That means that they must start looking for signs of boredom or restlessness before 2 minutes (which was the shortest length of independent play in the pretest assessment).

Dad initiated the plan by sitting down with Janet for a couple of minutes and playing with the blocks with her. When she was interested in the blocks, he moved away and began to "read." After 1½ minutes, he began to watch Janet for signs of boredom or frustration. As soon as she was restless, he went over and talked to her pleasantly and reinterested her in the blocks. He repeated this two more times, interesting her in a toy and a book, then stopped for the evening.

The next day Mother continued the program, beginning to watch for restlessness after 1½ minutes, and then progressing to 2 minutes. Janet played for at least 2½ minutes each time.

By the end of two weeks, they were up to seven minutes in a stretch with the parents in the room. But they could not leave the room or Janet would follow them. So they went back to the beginning and started leaving the room for brief periods and gradually built the length of time up.

The two preceding examples illustrate how shaping can be used for either simple or complex behavior. Shaping is a useful technique; however, it requires both planning and patience. Some parents wonder whether it is worth the time. In some cases, it is probably easier to put up with the problem; in other cases, the time involved in shaping a behavior needs to be compared with (1) the time lost over a several year period if the behavior is not changed, and (2) the degree of parental frustration resulting if the existing behavior remains unchanged.

Exercise 5-3: Shaping
Exercise 5-4: Concepts Needed for Learning

Exercise 5-3: Shaping

INSTRUCTIONS: *Assume that you have a small child who wants very much to put on her "long pants" but is having trouble. Divide the task of putting on pants into at least SIX small steps for her.*

1. _____

2. _____

3. _____

4. _____

5. _____

6. _____

7. _____

8. _____

POSSIBLE ANSWERS:
1. Spread pants flat on the floor.
2. Sit down at waist opening.
3. Slip each foot into waist and leg opening.
4. Pull each pant leg up so foot shows.
5. Repeat 3 and 4 with other leg.
6. Stand up and pull waist front up.
7. Reach in back and pull back up.

Relearn physical habits

Sometimes children forget to do things that they have done successfully before. You can jog their memory with *Redo-it-right* and *Over-learning*. These tools work best for physical habits and actions. The intention is to help children remember or relearn the desired actions, not to punish the children for forgetting.

Redo-it-right. This is a simple way to help the child get in the habit of doing something. For example, closing the front door or lowering the toilet seat. As soon as it is clear the child forgot, go to the child, put your arm around him and walk him back to where the child made the "error" so he can redo it right. As you go, explain what is happening. For example, "Oops, you forgot to close the door. I will help you." When you assist the child, remember to keep your manner pleasant and helpful.

I had a troop of twenty-four Brownie scouts. One rule in the building where we met was "No running inside." The girls were usually excited when they came in. Occasionally someone would forget and run to hang up her coat or talk to a friend. As soon as someone started to run, I would walk towards her. In the beginning of the year, I would put my arm around her and say, "Jenny, you forgot to walk. Let's go back and do it right." After a couple of weeks, all I needed to do was look up and the girl would turn around and go

Exercise 5-4: Concepts Needed for Learning

INSTRUCTIONS: Look at the steps involved in putting on pants (Exercise 5-3).
Decide what concepts or skills the child needs to be able to do them.

1. _____

   _____

2. _____

   _____

3. _____

   _____

POSSIBLE ANSWERS:

1. Understand concepts of in, front, and up.
2. Identify parts of pants and body.

3. Coordination to spread pants on the floor.
4. Physical control of hands and feet.

back. They had figured out that it took more time to go back and walk than to do it right the first time.

Over-learning is similar to redo-it-right, however in this technique the child repeats the action several times. A good way to learn a new skill is to practice it over and over again — whether it is stacking blocks, writing his or her name, or touching gently. This can be seen in the two stories below.

Becky was an energetic 16-month-old. She threw herself wholeheartedly into everything she did. When she saw baby kittens she tried to pet one with a pounding motion. I showed her how to pet gently. She would be gentle for a minute or two, and then slip back to the thump, thump, thump. After demonstrating again, I decided a longer learning process was needed. I sat down and put Becky in my lap, and a kitten in her lap. I would hold her hand for a couple of strokes and then let her pet the kitten. When she got too vigorous, I would take her hand and say, "Gently. The kitten likes it when we pet gently," as we stroked. Then I let her try again. After a couple of days she was able to pat gently without reminding.

When Martin was four he was fascinated with matches. If he found them, he was supposed to bring the matches to me, but sometimes he would strike them instead. Explaining how dangerous matches were seemed to make no difference. One afternoon I decided to teach him how to handle matches safely. I got a box of wooden kitchen matches. We made a fire-safe circle by removing twigs and leaves. I showed him how to strike the matches away from himself, and hold the flame up so it wouldn't burn his fingers. Once he had the idea, I made him strike and burn the whole box, one by one. It took a long time, but he hasn't struck a match since then. I think he now understands how to be safe and matches have lost some of their mystique.

Over-learning can be done as a part of the initial teaching process or as a consequence of forgetting. Whichever way — remember to approach the situation calmly and supportively, rather than being brisk or critical.

Problem solving skills

When conflicts arise between parents and children, parents can choose to look for solutions *with* the child. Two types of negotiation you can use with preschool children are: *A Better Way* and *Joint Problem Solving*. (Both approaches are presented in greater detail in my book *Kids Can Cooperate*.) If you choose to negotiate with a child, you need to consider the child's problem-solving ability. To be most effective at negotiations, a person needs to have some experience making decisions, thinking up ideas, and evaluating them. Since these skills come from experience, you may need to be patient when you begin.

A Better Way. The easiest way to start negotiations is to hunt for "A Better Way." You begin by stating what each person wants and then look for a better way. With a better way, you choose the first idea that you both agree upon. When you involve children in the problem solving process, they may come up with ideas that you would not have considered. The process is illustrated below.

Mornings were becoming the pits at my house. Amy (age three plus) wanted to dress by herself — which took forever. This particular morning I needed to hurry because I had an early meeting. When I tried to help her, she refused to let me. I considered picking her up and dressing her myself, but I knew it would be noisy and unpleasant and I would rather not fight just before the meeting. I also considered taking her as she was and letting her finish dressing at daycare. However, instead, I decided to try "A Better Way."

I described the problem to my daughter: "Amy, my way is to dress you now so we can leave. Your way is to dress yourself. What's a better way? A better way is something we both will like."

Amy thought a moment and then said, "Daddy do it?"

She asked him and he was willing. I would never have thought to ask him because I thought she wanted to do it by herself.

In this situation, Amy came up with a suggestion that worked for her mother. That will not always be the case. If your child offers an idea that is not acceptable, explain why and suggest the closest thing you can to the child's idea. This is a good technique to use if you are willing to consider new ideas, however if you know just what you want, try another approach.

Joint problem solving. As children become more experienced in thinking up and evaluating ideas, they can move to traditional problem solving where a variety of ideas are considered before choosing one. This is similar to the problem solving process described in Chapter 2. The difference occurs in how you begin. The steps are summarized in the word SIGEP: Stop, Identify, Generate, Evaluate, Plan. These are illustrated below.

Joint Problem Solving Illustration

Description:	Example:
Stop. When you are being drawn into a conflict with a child, stop. Calm yourself and decide how you want to continue. Otherwise conflicts can quickly escalate to unmanageable levels.	*(To child, age 4) Kelly, I told you "No." I can't play with you now. I am nursing the baby. Oops, I need to calm down. I'll take three deep breaths.*
Identify the problem & feelings. State what you want using underlying needs rather than a specific solution. (Helpful tip: use sentences that start with "I" and avoid words like "always" and "never.")	*Kelly, I feel frustrated because I need quiet time to nurse the baby. You feel angry or jealous that the baby has all my time. What can we do so you feel loved and I don't feel so frustrated?*
Generate ideas. Write down *all* ideas. Don't evaluate them yet. The more ideas you have to choose from, the more likely you are to find something that works for both you and your child. At a minimum, find one more than your child's age. (For example, five ideas with a four year old.)	Kelly: *You can leave the baby and play with me.* Mom: *I can watch as you do tricks. Or, you can watch TV till I'm done.* Kelly: *You can read as you nurse.* Mom: *I can play with you when I'm done nursing.*
Evaluate ideas. Read each idea and ask how each person feels about it. Star each idea that someone likes and cross out the ideas someone dislikes.	*We read and discussed the ideas one by one. Kelly wanted ideas where she could be with me immediately. I wanted ideas where I could continue to nurse. Fortunately, we agreed that I would read to her while I nursed the baby.*
Plan. Many good ideas fail because people do not make adequate plans. Think about who is responsible for activities, money, and schedule. Decide what you will do if something goes wrong.	*Our plan: Kelly will go get a book and I will read it to her. If the baby needs to burp or something, Kelly will wait while I care for the baby.*

In this situation Mom and Kelly were lucky. There was a simple solution they both accepted. If there are no ideas that work for both of you, go back to each of the ideas and ask the person who rejected it how it could be changed. The purpose of this approach is to find something that is agreeable to both parties. When child and parent agree, the solution is much easier to resolve.

In this chapter, we have seen that learning takes place best when the "teaching" is done when there are no problems, and provides concrete experiences for the child who is both developmentally ready and expecting to learn. Five specific tools or teaching methods presented were modeling, simple instruction, shaping, redo-it-right, and over-learning. As children grow older, you can teach your child to problem-solve difficulties with you. These skills can be added to those which increase acceptable behavior and help to avoid problem areas. Next we will look at techniques for decreasing inappropriate behavior.

Additional reading

Kids Can Cooperate, A practical guide to teaching problem solving by Elizabeth Crary. Parenting Press, Inc., Seattle, Washington, 1984.

Children's Problem Solving Series: *I Want It (1982), I Can't Wait, (1982), I Want to Play (1982), My Name Is Not Dummy (1984), I'm Lost (1985),* and *Mommy, Don't Go (1986)* by Elizabeth Crary. Parenting Press, Inc., Seattle, Washington.

▫ Each book focuses on a childhood problem, models the problem solving process, and offers possible solutions.

Dealing With Feelings Series: *I'm Mad, I'm Frustrated,* and *I'm Proud*, by Elizabeth Crary. Parenting Press, Inc., Seattle, Washington, 1992.

Chapter 6: Decreasing Inappropriate Behavior

Strange as it seems, it is usually easier and more effective in the long run to increase appropriate behavior than to decrease inappropriate behavior. However, there are times when parents want to do something concrete to decrease inappropriate behavior directly. At this point, it is often helpful for parents to decide the purpose of the child's misbehavior and specifically what they would want the child to do instead. Three techniques for changing inappropriate behavior move smoothly into increasing appropriate behavior. These are ignoring, substitution, and altering the environment. After discussing these, we will consider two techniques for dealing with more serious behavior.

Motives of misbehavior

Dreikurs, in his book *Children: the Challenge*, presents four motives for misbehavior or, in his terms, "levels of discouragement." He believes that all misbehavior stems from one of these four reasons: desire for attention, power, revenge, or display of inadequacy. The levels of misbehavior can be distinguished by what the child believes (probably unconsciously) about himself. Since parents are not mind readers, it may seem difficult to determine what the child believes about himself. Surprisingly, Dreikurs concludes that the motive of misbehavior can be inferred from the *parent's reaction* to the misbehavior, even though the same misbehavior might result from different motives.

Attention. The first level of misbehavior is desire for attention. Children choose this action when they believe they are worthwhile only when they receive attention. Attention-seeking behavior *annoys* the parents. When the child is reprimanded, she will stop immediately, but will frequently begin again later with the same or similar behavior. For example, after requested to "Keep your hands off the blinds," the child desiring adult attention may wait a few minutes then play with the blinds with her feet. Giving attention to *annoying* behavior will usually cause it to increase. The most constructive way to deal with bids for attention is to ignore the inappropriate behavior (see Ignoring, page 78), *and* increase attention at non-conflict times (see Focus Time, page 52).

Power. The second purpose of misbehavior is desire for power. Children seek power when they believe they are significant only when they are in control or are "the boss." Parents feel *anger* in response to power seeking behavior, and usually give in (child wins) or dominate (parent wins). Strangely, both of these responses contribute to the child's need for power by increasing its importance. The recommended response to bids for power is to "side step" the issue (by doing the unexpected) or by encouraging cooperation and mutual problem solving. Below is an example of avoiding a power struggle by finding a mutually agreeable solution.

Beth (2½) has refused to take her nap. Mother gave her the choice of sleeping in her crib or her big bed. Beth refused to do either. Instead of picking Beth up and putting her in bed or letting her stay up, Mother asked her, "Where do you want to sleep?" Beth replied, "Onna floor. In a sleeping bag." At this point Mother agreed and both were satisfied.

Revenge. Children sometimes turn to revenge when their needs for attention or power have not been satisfactorily met. Children who seek revenge adopt the position that they are significant only when they can hurt someone. Parents of a revengeful child feel *deeply hurt* by this behavior. The parents' usual response is to display their hurt and to retaliate in kind — only more strongly. When this happens, the whole child-parent relationship begins to suffer. The most constructive response for the parent is to refuse to act hurt, to devise ways to rebuild trust in the relationship, and to increase the child's feeling of being loved.

Display of inadequacy. Display of inadequacy is the last level of misbehavior. It can be viewed as the child's final triumph. The display of inadequacy may be confined to one area where the child feels she cannot succeed, or it may affect several areas. Such children feel alienated by the demands placed on them and feel acceptable only when no demands are made of them. The parents of an inadequate child feel *despair and hopelessness*. The most common response is to give up completely and pity the child. The most constructive response, however, is to stop *all* criticism and to reinforce *any* positive behavior.

As mentioned above, it is not always possible to tell the motive for misbehavior from the behavior alone. For example, hitting another child could result from a desire for attention, power, or revenge. Ignoring the hitting, if the purpose was for attention, would be successful; but if the purpose was for power, it would probably lead to an increase in hitting if it were perceived as successful.

Although the purposes of misbehavior are listed in four levels, Dreikurs believes a child can go directly from desire for attention or power to display of inadequacy. A pampered child, for example, who did not receive enough attention might adopt the position that she was totally useless.

Some parents find considering the motives of misbehavior very helpful; others object for philosophical or practical reasons. In either case, the motives of misbehavior may offer parents valuable insight. The remainder of this chapter presents specific techniques to help parents deal with unacceptable behavior. Modifying the environment focuses on changing things to reduce future trouble, while the other techniques present possible ways for the parent to respond when misbehavior occurs. If you find that considering motives of misbehavior is helpful, you may wish to reflect on how effective the various techniques would be for the different levels.

Exercise 6-1: Identifying Motives of Misbehavior

Exercise 6-1: Identifying Motives of Misbehavior

INSTRUCTIONS: Read the parent description of the situations below and decide how the parent felt and what the child's motive for misbehavior was. (Possible answers on following page.)

1. "Danny has always been an independent little boy. However, recently things have been getting worse. For several days he has been clamoring to ride his trike to Joey's alone. Joey lives at the end of the next block, and although there is not much traffic, I still don't feel comfortable with his going by himself."

    "Well, yesterday he went by himself even though he had promised to stay on our block. I was so mad I brought him home immediately and put his trike in the attic of the garage so he could not ride it again. While I was putting the trike up, he went out and took the blossoms off all the flowers he could reach. I was crushed! I was planning to use some of them in a display for the garden club next week, and he knew that. Why did he do something so vile?"

    Motive of misbehavior: _____

    Parent's feeling: _____

2. "I don't know what has come over Lari. She has become such a nuisance. Yesterday, while I had company, she asked me to read her a story. Usually I don't mind reading her a story, but yesterday I wanted to talk with my friend. I told her nicely that I would read her a story when my friend left. Next, she took off her clothes and started to go outside. I don't mind her being naked inside, but not outside. So I had to stop talking with my friend, bring her back, and help her put her clothes on so she could go outside."

    Motive of misbehavior: _____

    Parent's feeling: _____

3. "Zac is so stubborn, sometimes I don't know what to do. Yesterday, for example, he had played outside all afternoon and should have been hungry. But would he eat? No! I explained that he needed food to grow strong muscles and bones, but he refused to eat. I changed tactics and told him if he didn't eat, he couldn't have any dessert. He replied, 'So what? I don't want any. And I won't eat the yucky old meat loaf anyway.' Then I got really angry and told him, 'Listen, young man, you stay at the table until your plate is clean.' He started eating then, but ate very slowly. I had to keep him at the table half an hour after everyone else left."

    Motive of misbehavior: _____

    Parent's feeling: _____

4. "Annette used to be a lot of help, not perfect, but she would try. She dressed herself, and she could get something for me if I needed it. I don't know what has come over her, but she can't do anything anymore. I have to dress her, wipe her bottom if she remembers to go potty, or help her change her pants if she doesn't. She can't remember to do anything. It's almost like having a baby again. I've tried everything I can think of to make her act her age, but it's hopeless. Nothing works. I hope she grows out of it."

    Motive of misbehavior: _____

    Parent's feeling: _____

Distraction   The easiest time to teach compliance is when children are very little. If they misbehave you can either distract them or remind them of the rule and help them comply. When you follow through promptly (with only *one* reminder) you get children in the habit of complying. Distraction can be either simple or indirect.

Simple distraction. It involves interrupting the child's thought and redirecting it where you would like it to be. With simple distraction, if your son was crying, you could distract him with his favorite truck. Or if your daughter was headed toward Aunt Mary's shelf of glassware, you could distract her by pointing out the kitty. Distraction is a wonderful tool that children outgrow all too soon, so use it while you can. However, if every time your child heads for the VCR you distract her with a story, she may learn to use the VCR to get attention. If you notice an increase in a behavior that you are using distraction for, you can switch to indirect distraction.

Indirect distraction is similar to simple distraction; however, instead of talking to your child directly, you get his or her attention indirectly. You do something that draws her attention to you. While you try to distract them, avoid eye contact. Keep your back to them and ignore them. Here are two examples.

Annalee and I loved music. When she was little, I used the piano to draw her out of tantrums without giving the tantrums my attention. When I felt they went on long enough, I would go into the living room and start playing a march or some lively song. Before I could finish the first piece, she would be on the bench beside me.

When Robbie did not get what he wanted, he would pout. Normally this did not bother me, but last week it really got on my nerves. When I felt myself getting bent out of shape, I needed to do something constructive before I exploded. I remembered indirect distraction. Since he likes trucks, I took the fire engine and two shoe boxes that were out and made a lot of noise as the fire engine rushed to the fire. Just moments later he was beside me asking if he could play, too.

Distractions work well when you have a little time. However, if you want to encourage compliance or if the child is doing something dangerous to himself or someone else, you may need to physically assist the child to comply.

POSSIBLE ANSWERS for Exercise 6-1:

1. Danny: Motive - revenge. Parent's feeling - deeply hurt

2. Lari: Motive - attention. Parent's feeling - annoyed

3. Zac: Motive - power. Parent's feeling - anger

4. Annette: Motive - display of inadequacy. Parent's feelings - despair, hopelessness

---

Assisted compliance

Assisted compliance involves physically helping your child comply with your request. It is one of three parts to setting effective limits. The three parts are: a clear rule or command, a choice, and the follow through (assisted compliance). You will need to use the process differently depending on whether the child's situation is dangerous or not.

Dangerous situations. In dangerous situations, give a clear command, physically intervene, and then offer a choice of how to do better in the future. This can be seen in the following example.

Angie had an instinct for finding unsafe things. For example, one time when I was slicing apples, I put down the knife for just a moment to pick up a piece of apple I knocked on the floor. In a flash, Angie was on the counter reaching for the knife. I said "Stop!" and reached for her. When she was back on the floor I squatted at her level and said, "Knives are dangerous. I can't let you play with a knife. You can look at a knife while I hold it, or you can play with a plastic knife."

Sometimes parents intervene in dangerous situations, but neglect to satisfy the child's curiosity. Easy children will usually accept that. However, persistent children will often try repeatedly until you either satisfy their curiosity or exhaust their energy. It is usually easier to think of safe ways to satisfy their curiosity. Substitutions (later in this chapter) will help you find possible solutions.

Safe situations. In safe situations, remind the child of the rule or give a request. If your child does not respond promptly, offer a guided choice (in Chapter 3), then follow through with assisted compliance if needed. For example, when you say, "Chairs are for sitting on," and the child does not move, offer a guided choice, "You may sit down or get off the chair." If the child does not move, assist him to comply. Simply pick the child up and put him on the floor. He may scream or wiggle, but that is okay since you have not hurt him. The more consistent you are, the less you will have to intervene in the future.

Molly loves jumping. She always has. She used to pull herself up and bounce in the crib. When she learned to climb on the sofa she wanted to bounce there. It took about a week to redirect her. At first, when she jumped on the sofa I said, "The sofa is for sitting on. You may sit on the sofa or jump on the floor." She continued to jump so I put her on the floor. I reminded her, "You chose to jump on the floor." For the next couple of days she checked out jumping on the sofa. Every time she jumped on the sofa, I gently but firmly put her down and reminded her that the sofa was for sitting. It lasted less than a week. She hasn't jumped on the sofa for months.

Remember — before you make a rule or command, you must be willing to follow through. Persistent children may test the rule many, many times. The time you spend when they are young will save you many times over as the children grow older. However, some children may test limits as a way to get attention. If your child is "getting the message," the frequency or intensity of testing should begin to decline. If the frequency increases steadily after the first couple of times, your child may be using the behavior as an attention getter. If that is the case, ignore the behavior (described in this chapter) and work on encouraging positive behavior (Chapter 4).

Ignoring Most children have some habits that, while not "serious" in the sense that they are dangerous or destructive, are annoying. Ignoring is a good technique to try with these behaviors. As you recall from the section on increasing positive behavior (Chapter 4), if a behavior is not reinforced occasionally, it will decrease. So, if you *want* a behavior to stop or decrease in frequency — *ignore* it. The catch is, however, that you must ignore the behavior *every time* it occurs if you want it to go away. For example, if your toddler has picked up a "bad" word that you don't want him to use, you can ignore it. Do not respond to it at all. It will often die out by itself.

Sometimes if you wish to ignore a behavior, but it is very difficult, it may be necessary to physically absent yourself from the child's sight. This should be done as naturally as possible so it does not appear as the result of the child's behavior.

When parents begin a different response, such as ignoring, to an existing problem, they often find an increase in the unacceptable behavior rather than the expected decrease. This increase in negative behavior has been likened to the common reaction to an uncooperative vending machine. This is illustrated in the example below.

Bonnie put a quarter in a vending machine, pulled the knob, and nothing happened. She pulled the knob several more times and then pushed the coin return. When the coin return failed, she pulled the knob again and again with increasing vigor. Next she pounded on the machine a couple of times — still with no results. Then she pulled the knob one final time before giving up.
If a machine refuses to give the merchandise or return the coin, the person will give in eventually. If the machine had given the expected response (food or money) during one of the pounding or pulling sprees, Bonnie would have assumed that her actions had dislodged whatever was causing the problem. Children may also attempt to get the response they expect from their parents by increasing the intensity of their actions. If the child whines, he may whine more loudly or persistently than formerly, hoping to get the predicted response. If the parent can remain unresponsive, the inappropriate behavior will die out.

If you have difficulty ignoring whining or crying behavior, another alternative is to attempt to indirectly interest the child in something else. This is done by picking an activity that you think the child would like, and start playing by yourself. Let your enthusiasm and interest in the activity draw the child. *Do not* look at the child or try to involve him or her in any direct way. If you look at the child, you will probably reinforce the inappropriate behavior with your attention.

Ignoring works well as long as the unacceptable behavior is not being reinforced by anyone or anything else. But there are some behaviors so irritating to parents that they will give in eventually if the behavior persists. If you know you will give in eventually, then don't try to ignore the behavior. The occasional reinforcement (the eventual giving in) will strengthen the very behavior you are trying to eliminate.

In some cases, the behavior is not reinforced from the outside (i.e., by the parent), but rather from within the child. This is sometimes the case with thumb sucking, and banging toys to make loud noises. The child likes the way it feels or sounds and will continue with the behavior for his own sake. When a behavior is reinforced from within, ignoring alone will not decrease it. However, ignoring can be accompanied by reinforcing or teaching a behavior to replace the unacceptable one.

Substitution

Substitution replaces an inappropriate expression of an activity with an appropriate expression of the same activity. Substitution shows a child where and how to perform the same activity acceptably. For example, banging on the wall with a wooden hammer is not appropriate, but banging on a pounding bench with the same wooden hammer is appropriate; or, riding a tricycle in a crowded room may not be acceptable, while riding the same tricycle in the basement would be fine. In both examples, the activity was permitted, but redirected to acceptable channels.

You can change either the "tool" used or the "location" of the activity when you make a substitution. When Ricky banged on the wall with the wooden hammer, his mother chose to change the location (he was moved to the pounding bench) rather than the tool. However, she could have offered him a stuffed toy (substituted the tool) and permitted him to continue banging on the wall. When you free your imagination, many substitutions are possible in the same situation. Some substitutions will be acceptable to one person, but not to another. Keep looking until you find a substitution that is really okay with you.

After you have redirected the child's activity, it is wise to positively reinforce the acceptable behavior (see Chapter 4) several times to insure that the child has the right idea.

Exercise 6-2: Making Substitutions

One problem with the use of substitution for very young children is that it seldom solves the problem with the first use. A bright child, after finding that she should not hit the wall with the hammer in the morning when Mommy is around, may test to see if the rule holds when Daddy is around, with Mommy in the evening, or if perhaps hitting the door or the lamp with the hammer is acceptable. If the parent is calm, firm, and persistent, the substitution will soon be accepted. The testing period that often accompanies substitutions is easier to accept if it is viewed as a sign of curiosity and thinking ability, rather than as deliberate disobedience.

Substitution is different from distraction. Distraction attempts to interrupt the unacceptable behavior, but does not indicate how that activity may be carried out, nor does it respond to the child's interests. Distraction

Exercise 6-2: Making Substitutions

INSTRUCTIONS: Read the situations below and decide on the substitution you would make.

1. Mike (2½) has a screwdriver and is currently taking apart the living room lamp.

   _____

2. Mary (1½) has bitten the neighbor's child and is about to bite him again.

   _____

3. Peter (2) is scribbling in your book with a pencil.

   _____

4. Carrie (15 mo.) has just pulled all of Daddy's books from the shelf.

   _____

5. Paul (1½) wishes to help you put away the groceries by putting away the eggs.

   _____

6. Penny (18 mo.) is scribbling on paper with a permanent marking pen.

   _____

POSSIBLE SOLUTIONS:

1. *An old clock that is not working right instead of the lamp.*
2. *Give Mary a frozen teething ring to bite instead of the child.*
3. *Substitute a notebook for the book.*
4. *Move your daughter to her books, rather than Dad's.*
5. *Substitute the cans for the eggs.*
6. *Substitute crayons or washable marking pens for the permanent pen.*

may be appropriate when a child is quite young and exploring everything indiscriminately; however, when the child begins to seek out certain activities because he or she wants them, then distraction loses its effectiveness.

Substitution can be viewed as the beginning of problem solving. However, with substitution, the responsibility for determining needs, generating possible solutions, and selecting and implementing solutions falls on the parent. Substitution recognizes both the child's need for exploration and independence and the parent's need for safety and order. When the substitution is chosen wisely, both the parent and the child win. As the child becomes

Without Spanking or Spoiling

more verbal, his role in problem solving increases. The process of problem solving is presented in Chapter 5. Children's books that you can use are listed at the end of that chapter.

Modifying the environment

There are times when the activity that the child is pursuing cannot be suitably redirected. Many of these situations can be resolved by modifying the environment. For example, if your daughter is pulling the leaves off a potted plant, it is not likely that you would wish to substitute another plant or let her remove the leaves from the same plant in another room. However, you could modify the environment by hanging the plants or setting them beyond her reach. There are three general ways to modify the environment: adding to the environment, limiting the environment, and changing the environment.

Adding to the environment. We can add to the environment both by introducing materials or activities that interest the child and by broadening the areas in which the child may play. When I talk on the phone, I often bring out a toy or activity that my toddler has not seen for a while. One might have a special box of telephone or rainy-day toys. This could be acquired without additional expense by taking the toys the child is currently tired of, or not interested in, and putting them away for several weeks. Later, when the child needs to be occupied, some of these toys can be removed from storage.

When the child or parent becomes restless, it is often helpful to enlarge the environment by taking a trip to the park, pet shop, museum, or even a walk around the block. Enlarging the environment increases the area where the child can play.

Limiting the environment. We can limit the environment both by reducing the options and by restricting the space. Reducing the options involves stopping the activity or removing the stimulus. One may wish to reduce the child's options before bedtime or when the child has trouble concentrating on something (like eating). For example, Andy's father used to put him in his pajamas and roughhouse with him until bedtime. After roughhousing, it was almost impossible to put Andy to sleep because he was so excited. The environment was limited by replacing the roughhousing with reading stories, and bedtime became much easier.

The environment can also be limited by restricting the location of certain activities. Loud noises and rough play could be restricted to the basement; play dough, to a table; and eating, to the dining room.

Changing the environment. The environment can also be reorganized to encourage or discourage certain behavior. The environment can be changed either by simplifying things (providing the child appropriate facilities) or by rearranging items within the environment. Providing the child appropriate facilities (like low clothes hooks) encourages the child to function independently and effectively. A step stool by the sink, low towel bar in the bathroom, and child-size chairs all permit the toddler to act independently.

Space can be reorganized to make life easier for both toddlers and their parents. It is easier to find a toy on a toy shelf than in a toy box. A clothes basket in the child's room (or where she changes clothes) will be used more than one elsewhere. Televisions, stereos, and other instruments with inviting knobs can be put up high to reduce the temptation for small people. Safety equipment, like electrical outlet safety caps and drawer latches, can be installed to make the area safer. In these and other ways, your home can be changed so that the number of conflicts is reduced.

Exercise 6-3: Modifying the Environment

Ignoring, substitution, and altering the environment are all useful for decreasing inappropriate behavior. To be most effective, however, the tools must be accompanied by positive reinforcement of appropriate behavior when it occurs. In some situations, the child's behavior is so disruptive or dangerous that it must be stopped immediately. Two techniques to use in these situations are "consequences" and "time-outs."

Choosing appropriate consequences

Dreikurs offers two ways to decrease inappropriate behavior which he calls "natural consequences" and "logical consequences." With both of these methods, the results (or consequences) of the child's actions are clarified for the child before he chooses to act.

Natural consequences. Natural consequences are the inevitable results of the child's own actions. For example, if the child does not come to dinner on time, his dinner will get cold. Dreikurs terms this a "natural consequence" — a consequence which follows naturally from the child's action without parental intervention. Another example would be a child touching a hot stove after being warned — the consequence is that the child will get burned.

There are two advantages to using natural consequences. First, they permit children to be responsible for their own actions rather than protected from the results of them. Second, the natural consequences are not administered by the parent.

Logical consequences. In some cases, such as playing with an electrical outlet, the natural consequences are not inevitable or may be so severe as to be harmful. In these cases, Dreikurs offers "logical consequences." Logical consequences also follow from the child's action but necessitate parental intervention. For example, the "natural consequence" of running in the street will be nothing or being hit by a car. Nothing happening does not discourage the child from running in the street and being hit is unacceptable. A "logical consequence" of running in the street could be removal from the front yard and returning to the house.

Exercise 6-4: Identifying Consequences

To be effective, logical consequences must be applied each time the event occurs, must be logically related to the event, and must be truly acceptable to the parent.

The consequence for a behavior must occur each time the behavior does, or the omission must be explained. For example, if your child is warned that she must "play with the dog gently or the dog will go away," then every time the child plays roughly, the dog must be put in the basement or let

Exercise 6-3: Modifying the Environment

INSTRUCTIONS: For each situation below, write three ways to modify the environment.

Situation

A. Child riding a trike in a crowded living room.

1. _____
2. _____
3. _____

B. Child playing with the TV controls.

1. _____
2. _____
3. _____

C. Child digging in the flower box and disturbing the plants.

1. _____
2. _____
3. _____

D. Two children squabbling over one toy repeatedly.

1. _____
2. _____
3. _____

E. Child wishing to dress, but having trouble with a turtle-neck shirt.

1. _____
2. _____
3. _____

POSSIBLE ANSWERS:

A. Child riding trike in a crowded room.
1. *Take trike outdoors.*
2. *Restrict trike to basement.*
3. *Remove some furniture to make more room.*

B. Child playing with TV.
1. *Provide child with an old TV set.*
2. *Put TV in parents' room.*
3. *Put TV in playpen out of child's reach.*

C. Child digging in flower box.
1. *Get a sand box.*
2. *Take child to the beach.*
3. *Give child a toy.*

D. Two children squabbling over a toy.
1. *Remove toy from children.*
2. *Get a duplicate toy.*
3. *Take children on a walk.*

E. Child wishing to dress.
1. *Get elastic neck top.*
2. *Remove all difficult shirts.*
3. *Get a buttoned shirt.*

Exercise 6-4: Identifying Consequences

INSTRUCTIONS: Read each situation and then put an N in front of responses that are a "natural consequence," and an L before those that are "logical consequences."

Situation 1

Your daughter's room is so messy that you cannot walk anywhere without stepping on something.

_____ a.   "When the room is this messy, toys get broken because they get stepped on."
_____ b.   "When toys are left on the floor overnight, they 'disappear' for several days."
_____ c.   "When toys are left on the floor, they cannot be found when they are wanted."
_____ d.   "When the floor is so messy, Mom and Dad will not come in, even if they are called."

Situation 2

Your son dawdles with his dressing each morning so that he is not ready to go to nursery school when you leave.

_____ a.   "If you are not dressed by 8:00, you will have to go to nursery school in your pajamas."
_____ b.   "If you are not in your clothes, you will need to ride in the back seat so you can have more room to put on your shoes and socks while we drive." (Child prefers the front seat.)
_____ c.   "If you are not dressed in time, you will miss breakfast."

Situation 3

Your son has a pair of walkie-talkies. He keeps bending the antennas back and forth. You cannot afford to buy another pair if the antennas break.

_____ a.   "If the antennas get bent again, it will have to rest on the shelf for a day."
_____ b.   "If the antennas get bent enough, they will break off."

ANSWERS:

Situation 1: a-N, b-L, c-N, d-L
Situation 2: a-N, b-L, c-N
Situation 3: a-L, b-N

outside. If the child is permitted to play roughly with the dog sometimes, then the effectiveness of the consequence will be greatly reduced.

When parental intervention is necessary, the parent will be most effective by acting firmly, calmly, and predictably — like the pull of gravity. A parent can also explain to the child that his or her own behavior tells the parent what the child has decided. For example, if the consequence of running into the street is going inside and the child goes into the street, the parent can say, "I can see by your behavior that you have decided to go inside." Pleas and promises of better future behavior should be ignored. If the child has a tantrum, as sometimes happens the first couple of times consequences are used, ignore them and continue with the consequence.

Logical consequences need to be related to the inappropriate behavior or to the desired behavior in an obvious manner. For example, Father did not want his daughter to stand in her high chair. He told her, "The chair is for sitting. You may sit in your chair or stand on the floor." However, to have

Without Spanking or Spoiling

said, "Sit in the dinner chair, or stand in the chair and have no story after dinner," would not be clearly related to the behavior. When a result is not clearly related, it appears like a punishment rather than a consequence.

The logical consequence offered to a child must also be acceptable to the parent. For example, a mother and son were about to go out for a walk and the coat closet was blocked by a train made of a row of chairs. If Mother was willing to stay home, she could say, "Put the chairs back so we can get our coats out or we will have to stay home." However, if she has a doctor's appointment to keep or feels they both need a walk to keep their sanity, then that response would not be effective. Instead of being a consequence, it would be a meaningless threat, because the parent would not be willing or able to carry through. Children frequently have a way of calling adults' bluffs. In another example, suppose that mother was tired of picking the blocks off the floor. She could tell the children, "Pick the blocks up, or leave them on the floor and I will throw them out." This would be appropriate if she really was willing to throw them out, but most parents are not. A more effective consequence for most parents would be, "Pick up your blocks, or I will pick them up and give them a rest." (In this case, a "rest" is a period of time on a shelf out of sight.)

When parents choose consequences they can calmly and consistently enforce, applying consequences becomes a more effective tool with time. The three most common errors in using consequences are choosing results (1) that are not logically related to the "problem," (2) that are not really acceptable to the parent, or (3) permitting oneself to be diverted by tantrums or promises of better behavior. In the next exercise, you will have the opportunity to identify some errors in proposed consequences and to construct some more effective ones. After that we will look at the use of time-outs.

Exercise 6-5: Making Effective Consequences

Time-out

A time-out is a technique used to interrupt unacceptable behavior by removing the child from whatever reinforcing events are encouraging and strengthening the unacceptable behavior. Because of the complex nature of time-outs, they are more suited to preschoolers (3-5 years) and up, rather than toddlers. An adaptation appropriate for toddlers (tiny time-outs) is described later. A time-out should be viewed as a calming device rather than as a form of punishment. The time-out should be short enough to allow the child to go back to the original situation and practice appropriate behavior. Several short time-outs are better than one long time-out since they offer the child more opportunities to learn. When a child returns to the situation, indicate what is appropriate behavior and praise the child as soon as he or she begins to do it. Remember to praise the child later if he continues to do well.

The general procedure for using a time-out can be summarized in five steps: (1) explain what a time-out is and when it will be used (for what infraction), (2) walk the child through a time-out when it occurs, (3) time the

Exercise 6-5: Making Effective Consequences

INSTRUCTIONS: Read the situations and responses below. Each response has an error that makes it less effective as a consequence.   A. Identify the error.
        B. Write a more effective consequence.   *(Possible answers on page 87.)*

1.   Situation: Alan will not return Brian's truck when it is time for Brian to go home.
     Response: "Alan, give Brian his truck, or he will never come back again."

     Error: _____

     Consequence: _____

     _____

2.   Situation: Eric is about to hit his little sister.
     Response: "Play gently with your sister, or no *Sesame Street* this afternoon."

     Error: _____

     Consequence: _____

     _____

3.   Situation: Mother is picking Mark up from daycare and he has ignored her request to go.
     Response: "You can come now, or I'll leave without you."

     Error: _____

     Consequence: _____

     _____

4.   Situation: Keith is pulling on the tablecloth at dinner.
     Response: "Do you want to let go of the tablecloth, or shall I spank your hand?"

     Error: _____

     Consequence: _____

     _____

5.   Situation: Kitty is resisting getting into her bed.
     Response: "Get into bed, or no story tonight."

     Error: _____

     Consequence: _____

     _____

Without Spanking or Spoiling

quiet time, (4) tell the child when the time-out is over, and (5) reinforce appropriate behavior when the child returns to the situation.

Introducing time-outs. In order to use time-outs correctly, your child needs to understand such concepts as quiet and waiting. In general, this degree of understanding comes between 2½ and 3½ years of age. After you have determined that your child can understand the concepts, you need to choose a location for the time-out.

The location for a time-out should be far enough from the general activity that the child will not be able to provoke others or get attention, but near enough that he can tell what he is missing. It should also be a dull place with nothing to do. The back hall might be good, or a chair in the play room that is blocked from the view of others (such as behind a sofa).

Next, explain the time-out procedure to the child carefully. This is best done before he breaks the rule again. The child should be told that each time he breaks a certain rule or refuses to stop doing certain kinds of things, he will be told to take a time-out. Explain that a time-out means that he will have to go to a quiet place (e.g., in the hall) and stay there *quietly* doing *nothing* until he is told to return.

You will need to "walk" a child through the time-out until he completely understands what a time-out is. To do this, take the child by the hand and explain matter-of-factly that he must stay on the stool (in this location) until you tell him he may come back. Usually one or two demonstrations are sufficient before you can use time-outs without explanations.

The child must remain in the location quietly for the desired length of time (usually less than a minute for young children). When the time is up, tell the child he may come back. The measured waiting time *begins* when the child is quiet. If he cries or whines for two minutes, then the total time might be 2½ minutes.

After the time-out is completed and the child is told he may return, encourage the child to return to the situation from which he was removed, and explain to him what behavior is appropriate. Praise the child as soon as he

---

POSSIBLE ANSWERS for Exercise 6-5

1. *Error: There is no real choice. Most parents are unlikely to let Alan keep Brian's truck even if Alan would rather have Brian's truck than Brian's future visit.*
   Consequence: "Alan, you may give Brian his truck or I will give it to him."

2. *Error: The result is not connected with the "cause."*
   Consequence: "Play gently with your sister, or play alone in your room."

3. *Error: The parent is unlikely to follow through with the proposed result and find a new daycare center for tomorrow.*
   Consequence: "Mark, you may walk to the car or I will carry you."

4. *Error: The result is unrelated to the "cause."*
   Consequence: "Do you want to let go of the tablecloth, or shall I take your hand off?"

5. *Error: The result is not related to the "cause."*
   Consequence: "It is time to get in bed. Shall Kitty do it or Daddy do it for you?"

---

begins to play acceptably. Remember to praise again if he continues to play appropriately. Several short time-outs are better for learning than one long one because the child has the opportunity to come back to the original situation and learn acceptable behavior.

After the first few times you should be able to tell the child matter-of-factly to take a time-out. Do not argue or talk with the child. If he whines or cries, remember to start timing after he has quieted. Parents must be consistent using the time-out procedure or the child will keep using the undesirable behavior thinking (or hoping) that he may get away with it "this time."

When a particular undesirable behavior appears again and again, it is often easier to eliminate it by "tuning in" to the situation that precedes it or that begins the chain of events, than by cutting that behavior off early with a time-out or some other technique.

Exercise 6-6: Identifying Errors in Time-Outs

Tiny time-out. The tiny time-out is useful for toddlers or sensitive children. It accomplishes the same general function as the time-out (interrupting the unacceptable behavior), but it does not isolate the child. To interrupt the unacceptable behavior, simply lift the child from the situation and set her down a short distance away. While you move the child, it is often helpful to give a short explanation like, "No hitting people." After you set the child down, return to the situation and comfort the other child or survey the mess. When the crisis is past, return to the first child, active listen (page 41) if the child is upset, and explain what could have been done instead or explain the future consequence of such behavior (see logical consequences, page 82). After the brief explanation, encourage the child to return to the situation and reinforce appropriate behavior. To see how this works, let us consider the example below.

Matt (age 2½) hit his sister (6 mo) on the head with a wooden hammer and was about to do it again. His mother stepped in and lifted him away, saying, "I can't let you hit Mary." Next she turned her attention to Mary and interested her in a toy. Then she returned to Matt and explained, "I can't let you hit Mary. If you are very angry with her, you can hit the sofa or come and tell me about it." She watched him as he returned to see what he would do. When he got himself a book to look at, she said, "I see you want to read awhile. That's fine." and returned to her project nearby.

Sometimes parents prefer to send (or take) their child to his bedroom when he is disruptive rather than to establish a special time-out place. This functions more like a consequence than a time-out because there are toys for the child to play with in his room, and children are usually permitted to come out when they are in control again. In most cases, this works well both to interrupt the inappropriate behavior and to help the child calm down. There are two possible problems for which parents should watch. First, the child may become afraid of his room or associate it with unpleasantness. Second, the child may like playing alone in his room and misbehave in order to be alone.

Exercise 6-6: Identifying Errors in Time-Outs

INSTRUCTIONS: Look at the situation below and list all the errors you can find.

Situation: The family was seated at the dinner table. Bobby provoked Jimmy, leading to silliness and interrupting the parents' conversation. Mother responded by pleading, "Come on, boys, stop fooling around and eat your dinner. If you finish your meal, you can have some ice cream for dessert." The silliness continued. Then Father yelled, "Shut up and eat, or you'll go to your rooms!" The silliness stopped for a few moments, but soon the boys were at it again.

Exasperated, Father dragged Bobby to the basement steps and yelled, "Take a time-out! Sit here until you have settled down!" Bobby yelled back, "I didn't do anything, Jimmy did!" Father responded loudly, "I don't care what he did. Now sit down and shut up!" The argument continued.

Finally Bobby capitulated by whining, "Okay, okay, I'll eat now." At this point, Father let him return to the table with the command, "Sit down and be pleasant!" When Bobby returned, Mother served Bobby his dessert. Soon the boys were bickering again.

Errors:

1. _____

2. _____

3. _____

4. _____

5. _____

6. _____

SOME POSSIBLE ANSWERS:

1. *Letting silliness continue for awhile before attempting to stop it.*
2. *Trying to bribe boys to stop silliness (see page 55 for a discussion of bribes vs. rewards).*
3. *Threatening the boys: "Shut up or I'll ..."*
4. *Not calmly telling Bobby to take a time-out.*
5. *Arguing with Bobby about what happened.*
6. *Omitting a quiet time (permitting return without a time-out).*
7. *Rewarding arguing and silliness with dessert.*

Common errors with time-out. *Using time-outs for everything.* Time-outs are most effective when used for only a few specific situations. *Waiting until you are angry to use time-outs.* Time-outs should be used immediately when the behavior occurs. *Talking to the child during time-out.* Ignore the child. *Failing to make the time-out a teaching tool.* When the time-out is over, return the child to the situation and remind the child of his or her choices. *Failing to give positive feedback.* After the child returns, look for positive behavior to praise. Remember, the purpose of time-outs is to teach, not to punish.

So far we have talked about methods for decreasing inappropriate behavior that offer the child a choice of actions or that meet both the parent's and the child's needs. Parents sometimes feel that by not using more forceful methods, they are abdicating their power. This is not true — parents always have the option to use power in any situation. However, parents who frequently use direct power to solve conflicts usually find that, as their children grow older, more force is needed to obtain the same results. The methods presented so far usually become more effective with time and consistent use rather than less effective. Some of the problems involved with using direct power or negative reinforcement are presented in the next section.

Negative reinforcement

WARNING

Use of negative reinforcement with your child
may backfire or may be harmful to your relationship.

Negative reinforcement suppresses the behavior which immediately precedes it. A negative reinforcer is something unpleasant or something that the child does not want. It may be something traditionally disliked, such as a spanking or scolding, or it may be something more subtle, like assistance when it is not wanted. It may seem strange, for example, that by *helping* a child to dress when he wants to do it by himself, we may be inadvertently teaching him *not* to put on his clothes. But the negative reinforcement suppresses the behavior it follows (in this case, trying to dress himself). It may also seem strange that spanking may actually increase undesirable behavior. This happens if that behavior is the child's most effective way of getting attention. As with positive reinforcement, there are no clear rules as to what will or will not be a reinforcer.

Dangers of negative reinforcement

Negative reinforcement may sound like the opposite of positive reinforcement — it is not! There are some very significant differences.

1. **Negative reinforcement does not teach the child what to do**. For example, a child who was yelled at after hitting his sister may know he is not supposed to hit her, but he does not know what he *may* do when he is very angry with her. The next time he gets angry at her, he may push her down instead of hitting her. The child will probably get yelled at again, but he still will not know what he may do when he is angry.

If a parent chooses to use negative reinforcement with a child, it is essential that the parent help the child learn what he should do in those situations. (See Increasing Appropriate Behavior, Chapter 4; and Teaching New Behaviors, Chapter 5.)

2. **Negative reinforcement often strengthens some associated undesirable behavior**. This seems contradictory, but an explanation should make it fairly clear. Two sets of learning experiences are usually going on at the same time when negative reinforcement is used. (1) Negative reinforcement suppresses the behavior that precedes it, *and* (2) positive

reinforcement strengthens any behavior that takes away the negative reinforcement. Consider the example below.

When Dan teases his sister, his father yells at him. The yelling negatively reinforces the teasing and Dan stops teasing his sister, but he begins to cry. Next, his father stops yelling after Dan has stopped teasing his sister. Dan's crying is now positively reinforced because his father stopped yelling just after Dan started to cry. With repeated occurrences, Dan may learn to cry to stop his father's yelling.

In this example, the negative reinforcement (yelling) for one unacceptable behavior (teasing) resulted in positively reinforcing another unacceptable behavior (crying). Or, put another way, Dan learned two things: (1) that teasing results in being yelled at, and (2) that crying stops his dad's yelling. The same ideas are diagrammed below for those who prefer visual presentations. **First**, the negative reinforcer suppresses the behavior that brings on the negative reinforcer:

$$A \atop teasing \quad \text{——brings on——>} \quad {B \atop yelling} \quad \text{——which decreases——>} \quad {A \atop teasing}$$

Second, removal of the negative reinforcer strengthens the behavior that removes it:

$$C \atop crying \quad \text{——takes away——>} \quad {B \atop yelling} \quad \text{——which strengthens——>} \quad {C \atop crying\ to\ remove \atop the\ adult's\ anger}$$

3. **Negative reinforcement often mars the parent-child relationship.** The child may fear, resent, or avoid the person(s) who punishes him. This is particularly true if the punishment is severe or appears severe to the child. When the child-parent relationship is disturbed in one area, it makes it more difficult for the relationship to function well in other areas. This means that all forms of guidance (modeling, substitution, grandma's rule, etc.) will work less effectively.

4. **Negative reinforcement will not change the behavior over a long time** unless the reinforcement is very severe or unless it is used *every* time. This means that your child will comply while you are present, but may do what he wishes when you are not around. Also, the child is very likely to revert to the behavior later if a new behavior has not been learned to replace the unacceptable one.

In any situation, a parent has the choice to use power to respond to conflicts that occur. A wise parent will weigh the benefits and the risks involved before using much power.

In this chapter, we have looked at eight techniques for decreasing inappropriate activities: distraction (simple and indirect), assisted compliance, ignoring, substitution, modifying the environment, consequences, time-outs, and negative reinforcement. No one technique will work all the time.

Techniques vary in effectiveness between children, and for the same child at different ages. In the next chapter, we will look at how to integrate these skills with those from the previous chapters to solve particular problems that occur.

Additional reading

Improving Your Child's Behavior by Madeline C. Hunter and Paul V. Carlson. Bowmar, Glendale, California, 1971.
- Chapter 3: Negative reinforcement
- Chapter 4: Extinction (Ignoring)

Parent Effectiveness Training by Dr. Thomas Gordon. Peter H. Wyden, Inc., New York, 1970.
- Chapter 8: Modifying the environment
- Chapter 10: Parental Power

Children: the Challenge by Rudolf Dreikurs. Hawthorn Books, Inc., New York, 1964.
- Chapter 4: The child's mistaken goals
- Chapter 6: Use of natural and logical consequences

Chapter 7: Putting It All Together

Parents often become accustomed to handling all situations in the same way, even if they are not really satisfied with the results. A sort of tunnel vision blinds them to many of the alternatives available because it is difficult to think of new or creative solutions in the heat of conflict. If a frustrating problem occurs time and again, take some quiet time and formally work the problem through the "solving steps."

In this chapter we will take two families' problems through the "solving steps" discussed in Chapter 2 and generate as many potential solutions as possible from the techniques presented in this book. A diagram of the procedure is presented on the following page.

First situation — as described by the parent (Nancy)

I am in the car taking my son Matt (age 3), his friend, and the baby (6 mo.) to the park. The boys are in the back seat, and the baby is in the front seat with me.

At first, the kids are talking happily. Then Matt reaches over and pokes his friend's leg. The friend says, "No," loudly and begins to whine. Matt pokes again. The friend yells and tells me he is being poked. I say to Matt, "Your friend doesn't want to be poked. Please keep your hands off." He continues to poke. I repeat, "Please stop!" He continues. I am frustrated and angry. Eventually, I reach back and slap Matt's leg.

Step 1: Define problem

Two possible specific behavior definitions of the problem suggest themselves for this situation.
A. The noise from the back seat was disturbing the driver.
B. One child was hurting the other child.

Step 2: Gather data

The situation Nancy described had happened several times, but she could not remember when it started. She thought it had not been too long. Because Nancy was driving, she was unable to see what happened in the back seat. Thus she did not know if the friend was provoking Matt in some way.

Who owns the problem? This problem could be owned by Nancy or by the children. The children would own the problem if Nancy felt either that children should learn to resolve their own differences or that her son's friend had invited the pokes by some silent taunts.

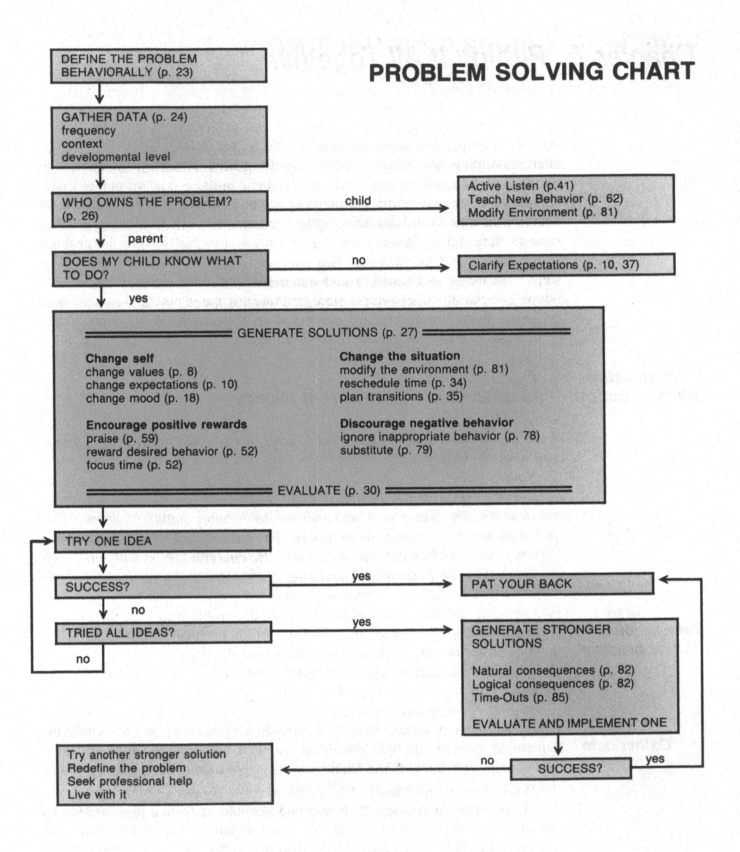

DEFINE THE PROBLEM BEHAVIORALLY (p. 23)

GATHER DATA (p. 24)
frequency
context
developmental level

WHO OWNS THE PROBLEM? (p. 26)

child →

Active Listen (p.41)
Teach New Behavior (p. 62)
Modify Environment (p. 81)

parent

DOES MY CHILD KNOW WHAT TO DO?

no →

Clarify Expectations (p. 10, 37)

yes

GENERATE SOLUTIONS (p. 27)

Change self
change values (p. 8)
change expectations (p. 10)
change mood (p. 18)

Change the situation
modify the environment (p. 81)
reschedule time (p. 34)
plan transitions (p. 35)

Encourage positive rewards
praise (p. 59)
reward desired behavior (p. 52)
focus time (p. 52)

Discourage negative behavior
ignore inappropriate behavior (p. 78)
substitute (p. 79)

EVALUATE (p. 30)

TRY ONE IDEA

SUCCESS?

yes →

PAT YOUR BACK

no

TRIED ALL IDEAS?

yes →

no

GENERATE STRONGER SOLUTIONS

Natural consequences (p. 82)
Logical consequences (p. 82)
Time-Outs (p. 85)

EVALUATE AND IMPLEMENT ONE

Try another stronger solution
Redefine the problem
Seek professional help
Live with it

← no

SUCCESS?

yes →

Nancy would own the problem if she felt that there was too much noise to drive safely, that people were not to be hurt under any circumstances, or that the friend was unable to defend himself. In this situation Nancy felt that her son should not poke his friend, so she classed it as her problem.

Does the child know what to do? At first, Nancy thought Matt should know what to do, she had "told him enough times not to hit his friend." However, upon reflection she realized that what she had told him does not really tell Matt what he *can do*, only what he *cannot do*. She decided she was willing for him to express his feelings, but not by poking. Nancy decided Matt could tell his friend how he felt or make a face to show how he felt.

Step 3: Generate solutions

We will now generate possible solutions using the categories as presented in the problem solving diagram (page 94). Some of the potential solutions may be pretty wild, but that is okay. The process of generating ideas should be completely separate from the process of evaluating them.

How can I change? Can I change my mood, values, or expectations so that the problem does not occur?

1. Have a nice cool lemonade or piece of chocolate cake before leaving for the park. (change mood)
2. Go away for a weekend without any children. (mood)
3. Decide it is okay for Matt to poke his friend. (values)
4. Decide that it is typical for this age, and it will pass. (expectations)
5. Decide it is really the friend's problem, and he should deal with it. (values)

How can I change the situation? Can I modify the environment, change activity, reschedule time, or plan transitions to decrease or eliminate the problem?

6. Move the children farther apart, or move one child to the front seat. (modify environment)
7. Put a barrier between the children: a large stuffed animal, a dog, a large pillow, a large cardboard box, etc. (modify environment)
8. Give the children something to occupy themselves with in the car: chalkboards, games, play dough, coloring books, etc. (modify environment)
9. Play a game or sing with the children while traveling in the car. (modify environment)
10. Go to the park after a nap while the children are refreshed, or after a meal while they are still pleasantly full. (reschedule time)
11. Go for a walk instead of a ride in the car. (modify environment)

How can I encourage positive behavior? In the preceding step, Nancy decided that Matt could make faces or talk. In addition, she would be willing for him to sing or count to ten. These could be reinforced with praise, M&Ms, or gold stars. Below are some ways to encourage specific behavior.

12. Encourage Matt to make faces by making faces, too.

13. Reward "talking" with a small bag of food to feed the ducks at the park.
14. Encourage singing by singing, too.
15. Have a treat available to give Matt when he uses an appropriate means to express himself.
16. Give him M&Ms (or crumbs for the ducks) for each attempt to count to ten.
17. Respond to making faces with, "Wow, you must really be mad!"
18. Play a rhyming game with the boys as long as they are pleasant.

How can I discourage inappropriate behavior? How can I use ignoring, substitution, or consequences to reduce the inappropriate behavior?
19. Do not respond to, or comment on, poking when it occurs. (ignore)
20. Have Matt poke himself instead of his friend. (substitute)
21. Have him poke the car seat. (substitute)
22. Have him poke a large stuffed animal. (substitute)
23. Have him poke the back of the front seat. (substitute)
24. Matt may sit in the back seat without hurting his friend, or he may sit in the front seat. (consequence)
25. Matt may go to the park without poking his friend, or Matt may go home. (consequence)

***Step 4:
Evaluate ideas,
pick one, and
implement it***

Now the time has come to evaluate the ideas and discard those that are too expensive, impractical, or are not compatible with your values or personality. If you have generated many ideas, then you probably have several ideas that are acceptable.

In this situation, Nancy felt that she could not change her values, but that she could change the situation easily. She decided to move Matt to the front seat and the baby to the back seat. That way there was no possibility for Matt to hit his friend. She did not move the friend to the front seat because then Matt could hit the baby instead.

***Step 5:
Evaluate
solution***

The solution worked. It did not teach Matt to control himself, but it did stop him from hitting his friend. Nancy hoped that when she put them together later, Matt would have gained sufficient control that he would not poke his friend. If for some reason the solution had not worked, Nancy could have chosen a new idea and tried it.

If none of the solutions worked, then Nancy would need to generate some new solutions. For example, she could say that each time Matt poked his friend, she would stop the car and let the boys out for a few minutes as a time-out. If there were too many time-outs, then there would be no time left for the park.

If none of the new solutions worked, Nancy would have the choice of redefining the problem, accepting (living with) the problem, or seeking professional help.

Second situation — as described by mother (Alice)

I have a problem I don't know what to do about. Regardless of how much planning I put in, something always happens each morning so I can't leave on time. Last Monday it was really important to me to leave on time, so I spent a good deal of time Sunday packing lunches, getting clothes ready, finding school stuff, and so on. Everything was going smoothly Monday until the last couple of minutes. During that time my son Adam (age 2 3/4) managed to take off his pants and shoes, lose his shoe laces, and distribute the packed lunches all over his sister's room.

Step 1:
Define problem

Adam delays our departure.

Step 2:
Gather data

The situation Alice described above happened about four times a week. Adam usually undressed and disrupted things when his mother was not in the room. Alice felt he was capable of occupying himself constructively and staying dressed for five minutes, since he did at other times during the day.

Who owns the problem? Alice decided that she owned the problem. Adam appeared happy, but her need to leave on time was not met.

Does the child know what to do? Alice thought Adam knew what to do since he could occupy himself constructively at other times during the day. But she commented that they had not talked specifically about what he could do in the morning while he was waiting for her.

Step 3:
Generate solutions

Next Alice and several friends generated possible solutions for her problem using the categories as presented in the problem solving diagram. Some of the potential solutions were rather wild, but that is all right. When the ideas generated do not have to be practical, it frees people to think creatively. The ideas will be evaluated later to see if they are acceptable.

How can I change? Can I change my mood, values, or expectations so that the problem does not occur?
1. Decide it is okay for Adam to go to the babysitter's with some clothes off or in his pajamas. (values)
2. Resign myself to having to redress him and clean up at the end, and plan my time that way. (expectations)
3. Refuse to be hassled or hurried by Adam's actions. (mood)

How can I change the situation? Can I modify the environment, change activity, reschedule time, or plan transitions to decrease or eliminate the problem?
4. Bring out a special toy for "waiting times." (modify environment)
5. Give him a nutritious snack to help keep him busy for the last few minutes. (change activity)

6. Give him Dad's old shoes to lace and unlace. (modify environment)
7. Keep Adam in the same room as Mom. (restrict environment)
8. Put mittens on his hands to slow him down. (restrict environment)
9. Put him in his car seat before turning out the lights. (restrict environment)
10. Tie the laces onto his shoes. (restrict environment)
11. Buy him slip-on shoes or sneakers with velcro. (change the situation)
12. Put boots over his shoes to slow him down. (restrict the environment)
13. Alice could get completely dressed and turn out all but one of the lights before dressing Adam. (reschedule time)
14. Alice could take Adam to the babysitter the previous evening if it was very important to leave on time. (reschedule time)
15. Alice could take Adam to the babysitter an hour early and then return home to finish. (reschedule time)
16. Mom could dress Adam first and feed him breakfast while doing last minute things. (reschedule time)
17. Mom could put lunches and other gear in the car the night before or earlier in the morning so it would not need to be done at the last minute. (reschedule time)
18. Give Adam some last minute jobs like turning out the lights. (reschedule time)
19. Give Adam a list of jobs to do while he waits. (plan transitions)

How can I encourage positive behavior? In the preceding steps we have generated some things Adam could do instead of undressing and spreading the lunches around. Below are some ways Alice could encourage positive behavior.

20. Praise Adam for cooperation.
21. Praise Adam for the clothes he has left on.
22. Give Adam a treat for each minute he remains dressed.
23. Give Adam a treat for each piece of clothing remaining on.
24. Plan to read him a story in the last five minutes if he is dressed and ready to go.
25. Sing with him as long as he remains dressed.

How can I discourage inappropriate behavior? How can I use ignoring, substitution, or consequences to reduce the inappropriate behavior?

26. Give him a life-size doll to dress and undress. (substitution)
27. Give Adam an extra snack that he can unpack and eat when he wishes. (substitution)
28. Pack his breakfast so that he can unpack it and eat it. (substitution)
29. Give him a gift-wrapped box to unwrap. (substitution)
30. Tell Adam, "If you don't have your shoes on when it is time to go, you will go without them." (consequence)
31. Tell Adam, "If you are not ready to go when I am, you will stay home with Grandma." (consequence)
32. Take Adam as he is when Mom is ready to leave without scolding or commenting on his attire. (ignoring and consequence)

Step 4:
Evaluate ideas,
pick one, and
implement it

Now the time has come to evaluate the ideas and discard those that are too expensive, impractical, or are not compatible with your values or personality. If you have generated many ideas, then several of them may be acceptable to you.

In this situation, Alice did not feel that she could change or that she could take Adam to the babysitter semi-clothed. She also disliked using food as a reinforcement. However, she could restructure her time or plan the transitions differently. As a first choice, she decided to give Adam some last minute jobs like turning off lights and seeing that doors were locked. If that did not work, she would plan to take Adam to the babysitter earlier and then come back for coffee and relax briefly before going to work.

Step 5:
Evaluate
solution

Planning a departure ritual helped reduce the number of delays. However, Alice felt she needed to check to see that there was something for Adam to do and found that a bit frustrating, but much less so than the previous scene.

Many potential solutions were generated for the example above. No one solution would suit every situation. The solution that is most effective for one combination of parent and child might not work for another. With experience, all parents can develop skills that are useful for them and their children. Often, as the children and parents grow, parents will need to revise and adapt their techniques to meet the changes.

As children grow older, it is important to remember that (1) they need to take a larger role in the problem solving process, and (2) they often try to control their parents in the same manner they have been controlled. Children who have been controlled primarily by power have the ultimate control in the teen years by running away from home. Children who have been shown constructive means of communication and problem solving in their early years have the means to develop solutions agreeable to both their parents and themselves.

A closing

Without Spanking or Spoiling offers thirty-two strategies or tools for guiding children. Some are simple, others are more complex and time consuming. These tools can be used informally for small concerns or more deliberately for larger problems. As you ponder what to do, consider both your temperament and your child's.

Reflect back on the "easy child" and the "difficult child" in Chapter 1 — appreciate the differences among children and their needs. Remember, no one tool works for everyone. Find the tools that work for you. If you have trouble finding effective tools, ask friends or professionals for help. If you know what to do and have trouble getting yourself to do it, get some help or support for yourself. As *you* learn and grow, you model growing for your child. And remember, children don't need perfect parents; they need loving, growing, persistent parents.

Appendix One:
150 Ideas for Common Problems

This appendix contains a problem solving summary, a problem solving planning sheet, and ten examples of how the tools in this book have been used to solve common problems.

- Bites
- Whines
- Fussy eater
- Throws things
- Won't pick up toys

- Fights diaper changes
- Screams when put in her car seat
- Dawdles, isn't ready in the morning
- Trouble getting kids to bed at night
- Won't sit still

You can use these ideas directly if you have the same problem and if the ideas appeal to you. Or, you can take these ideas and adapt them to your situation. For example, if you have trouble with your child sitting still in the doctor's office, you can use ideas from *Won't Sit Still*.

If your problem is very different from the ones above, you can use the examples as a guide for thinking up new solutions for *your* situation. There is no limit to ideas you can dream up. If you have trouble thinking them up, ask friends to help. When you generate new ideas, remember to jot them all down. If you stop to criticize the ideas or say why they won't work, you block the creative process. Later, after you have stopped thinking of ideas, you can decide which will work and which will not.

When you use the problem solving sheet to find ideas, you will notice that not all tools work equally well for all problems. This is because no one technique works all the time. Further, you may think of some ideas or approaches that are not included in this chart. Be sure to add them to your list.

After you generate ideas, you need to make a plan and revise it, if necessary. Remember, very few "people problems" are solved in a day. You need patience and persistence. To be effective in the long run, the plan must be respectful of both parent and child, and realistic for the temperaments involved.

Problem Solving Process

As children grow older, alternatives that worked well for one age may no longer be effective. Approaches that worked well with one child may have no affect on another. The sense of frustration a parent feels when techniques no longer work often has to do as much with the parent's feeling of incompetence as with the child's behavior. The more alternatives a person has, the more likely he or she is to find one that will work in any given situation.

Following are several ideas you can use to generate alternatives when your child's behavior is unacceptable. When you list ideas, do not limit yourself to "practical" ones. Often a really crazy idea will spark a truly good one.

1. Describe the problem:
Focus on behavior. What does the child do or say that is unacceptable? Avoid labels or generalizations. For example, "My child is rude," might become "My child interrupts when I am speaking."

2. Gather Data.

• **Record observations**: Log when and where the behavior occurs. Is it once a minute, hour, or day? Is it at certain times of day (before nap, before supper)? Does it occur more frequently with certain people or in particular places? This data may give you clues for how to handle the situation.

• **Decide who owns the problem**. Whose needs are not being met? Parent's, child's, both?

• **Decide what behavior you want the child to do** in place of the problem behavior. Think of specific actions you want your child to do, rather than general statements. It is unrealistic to expect your child to find acceptable behavior if the parent cannot. For example, "Don't interrupt," could become, "Put your hand on my arm and wait until I stop talking before asking your questions."

3. Generate alternatives.
The following are ideas you can use to generate alternatives. Remember, when you list ideas, do not limit yourself to "practical" ones. Silly ideas often stimulate really good ones.

• **Encourage desired behavior.** Common ways to encourage new behavior are praise, rewards (reinforcers), and noticing and acknowledging the effort a child makes to change. Decide on two ways to reinforce the behavior you want. For example, you could thank the child for waiting pleasantly and tell her, "Each time you wait patiently, I will read you a story."

• **Acknowledge feelings.** Reflect the feelings and content of the child's situation. Acknowledging feelings makes no judgment about the feeling and does not attempt to change it. For example, "You really want an ice cream cone and are disappointed you can't have one." Or, "You're furious your brother got to go fishing with Uncle Paul and you have to stay home."

• **List two ways to avoid the problem**. How can you change the environment or your behavior to avoid the problem? For example, have lengthy conversations when the child is asleep; hold your conversations in a sound proof booth; or, when the child appears, put her on your lap and tell her you will talk with her in just a moment.

• **Provide alternatives**. Offer your child several ways to get her needs met. One way to do this is to change the time, tool, or location of the activity. For example, "Do not interrupt. You may ask your dad for help (changing tool) or ask me when I am done (changing time)."

• **Establish consequences for unacceptable behavior.** Most children will test limits. You can make the process easier if you state in advance the consequence of testing. Effective consequences are: (1) related to the offending behavior; (2) ones the parent is willing to provide; and (3) delivered with low energy (not anger). For example, say calmly, "Jenny, you can wait quietly beside me, or go to your room. If you are noisy, I will take you to your room."

4. Make and implement a plan.
Choose an idea to try first. Consider your child's age and temperament, and your energy level. Consult all the people involved. Set aside ideas that are too expensive, too time consuming, or inconsistent with your values.

Plan your follow through. What will you do when your child tests the limits? Children learn more from actions than from words. When you tell a child to do something and do not follow through when she doesn't, you *teach* her to disregard you. When a child ignores a rule, remind her once, "Walk beside me or ride in the stroller," then if she runs away, pick her up and put her in the stroller.

5. Evaluate, revise, and repeat.
Few "people problems" are completely resolved on the first try. Track the behavior to see if it is getting better. If, after several days, the frequency does not decrease, then choose another idea. Continue revising your plan until you resolve the situation.

Problem Solving Planning Sheet

This sheet is a guide to brainstorming. Do not restrict yourself to ideas that are "reasonable."

1. Describe the problem. (Specific behaviors) _____

_____

2. Gather Data.

Record observations (five times). The behavior occurs about _____ times a day or hour.

It often happens when: _____

Who owns the problem? ☐ Child ☐ Parent ☐ Both

What behavior do you want? _____

3. Generate alternatives.

List three ways to **encourage desired** behavior. *(Praise, reward, smile, acknowledge effort)*

   1. _____

   2. _____

   3. _____

List one way to **acknowledge feelings**. *(Reflect feelings and content of the situation)*

   4. _____

List three ways to **avoid the problem**. *(Change environment—enrich, remove, rearrange; change schedule—time, sequences, transitions; A Better Way)*

   5. _____

   6. _____

   7. _____

List three **alternative** choices for the child. *(Change "tool," activity, place, or time)*

   8. _____

   9. _____

   10. _____

Determine **consequences** *(Natural or logical)*

   11. _____

   12. _____

4. Make and implement a plan.   First, I will try _____

I will explain my plan to my child by _____

If my child tests this plan I will _____

5. Evaluate, revise, and repeat.   I will try this approach for _____ *(days/weeks)*

If needed, I may try _____   or _____

Throws Things

Situation:

I have a major problem. My son, Ian (20 months), throws things. It wasn't so bad when he was smaller and threw plastic toys. Now he throws metal trucks, wooden blocks, and other toys. I am afraid he is going to break a window or hurt someone.

1. Describe the problem.

Ian throws heavy and hurtful objects.

2. Gather Data.

Record observations: He throws things a couple of times a day. However, on one day he was averaging more than three times an hour. It usually happens late in the morning or afternoon. I guess I own the problem since he is quite content to throw things.

Is throwing things typical for the age? Yes! Toddlers frequently experiment with dropping and throwing things.

What behavior do you want? I want him to throw something soft or do something else.

3. Generate alternatives.

Alternatives—Choices for the child.
- Say, "You can throw something soft." *(change tool)*
- Say, "You can throw blocks outside." *(change location)*
- Say, "You can read a book." *(change activity)*

Acknowledge feelings.
- Say, "You feel frustrated when I stop you from throwing things." *(active listening)*
- Say, "Looks like you feel mad and want to throw your trucks." *(active listening)*

Avoid the problem.
- Put the hard toys out of reach. *(items from environment)*
- Make bean bags and a target for him to throw at. *(add to environment)*
- Take him outside for a walk before lunch and dinner to run off energy. *(change schedule)*
- Pad the walls and remove furniture so he won't hurt anything. *(rearrange environment)*
- Tie the trucks to a chair so he can't throw them. *(rearrange environment)*

Encourage desired behavior.
- Smile and talk pleasantly with him when he throws the bean bag at the target. *(attention)*
- Say, "You remembered to throw a soft toy," when he switches from a heavy object to a soft one. *(praise)*
- Give him a star when he plays with the trucks appropriately. *(reward)*

Establish consequences.
- "Play with the toy appropriately (no throwing), or I will put it away for a week." *(logical consequence)*
- "Throw only the bean bag." Remove the toy he throws and give him the bean bag. Say, "Trucks are for driving. Bean bags are for throwing." *(logical consequence)*

4. Plan—make and implement a plan.

First, I will try substituting a bean bag for hard items. I will show Ian how to throw the bean bag at a target and acknowledge his efforts when he throws the bean bag.

5. Evaluate, revise, and repeat.

I will try this approach for four days. If it doesn't work, I will pick up the toy he throws and put it away for three days. If we are still having trouble a week later, I will generate new ideas.

Whines

Situation:

I can't stand whining. Whenever Matty (age 4) wants anything, she asks in a whiny voice. In the beginning, I tell her, "No!" but when she continues, I start screaming and eventually give in.

1. Describe the problem.

Matty whines when she wants something.

2. Gather Data.

Record observations: She whines mostly in the late afternoon. Several times a day. If I tell her "No," she waits a bit and then starts again later.

Is whining typical for the age? Yes. Many preschoolers have learned that if they ask pleasantly, they are ignored. However, if they whine, they get attention, even if the parent is angry.

What behavior do you want? I want her to ask pleasantly for what she wants.

3. Generate alternatives.

Avoid the problem or help her notice when she is whining.
• Notice when she is getting tired and do something fun or active. *(change schedule)*
• Ask her to get my attention *before* she makes a request. *(change sequence)*
• Ask her to get my attention by raising her hand or ringing a bell. *(change method)*
• If she whines, say, "Please repeat that, smiling." It is hard to smile and whine at the same time. *(attention and explaining what you want)*
• Ignore the whining. Leave the room if necessary. *(ignore)*
• Tell her, "You may have one whine a day." In the morning give her a "Whine Card." Then if she whines, ask her if this is her one whine. If so, she must give you the card, otherwise she needs to ask pleasantly. If she wants something fast, she may learn that it is quicker to ask pleasantly.

Encourage desired behavior.
• Listen and respond when she talks pleasantly. *(attention)*
• Say, "I like the voice you are using." *(praise)*
• Give her what she asks for when she speaks pleasantly. If you can't, acknowledge why you can't do what she wants and offer her something else instead. *(reward)*

Acknowledge feelings.
• Say, "When I hear people whine, I feel grumpy and I don't want to cooperate." *(I-message)*

Alternatives—choices for Matty.
• Say, "You may speak pleasantly." (change tool)
• Say, "Sing your request." *(change the activity)*
• Say, "Whine in the bathroom—alone." *(change location)*

Establish consequences.
• Say, "If you whine, the answer is *No*." *(logical consequence)*
• Say, "I will not listen to whining. If you whine, I will ask you to repeat the question pleasantly." Then ask her to do so. *(logical consequence)*

4. Plan——make and implement a plan.

I will explain, "I want you to talk pleasantly. If you whine, the answer will be an automatic "No." But you may ask again, pleasantly, three minutes later."

5. Evaluate, revise, and repeat.

I will try this for one week. If it doesn't work, I will ask her to get my attention before making any request. If she whines, I will ask her to repeat the question until she does it pleasantly.

Dawdles in the Morning

Situation:

Mornings are maddening. I feel like a shrew by the time Mark (age 4) is dressed. No matter how many times I remind him, he is never ready on time. I always end up helping. As long as I am there, he concentrates; as soon as I am gone, he gets distracted.

1. Describe the problem.

Mark is not ready to go to preschool on time in the morning.

2. Gather Data.

Record observations: I had to sit with Mark four out of five mornings this week.

Is this typical for the age? Emphatically, yes. In my book *Pick Up Your Socks* there is a chart showing that the *average* age children dress themselves when reminded or supervised is five years old. The *average* age they dress without reminders is over ten years old.

What behavior do you want? I want him to be ready on time (9:00 AM) without prodding from me.

3. Generate alternatives.

Change parent's attitude.
- I will sit with him, since children usually need support. *(change expectations)*
- I will happily sit with him since all too soon he won't want me "butting in" his life. *(change frame of reference)*
- I will look for what he has done and praise it, rather than what he has not done. (change attitude)

Encourage desired behavior.
- Sit with him as long as he is dressing. When he stops, leave the room. *(attention)*
- When I go in and find he has one sock on say, "I'm glad you have started putting your socks on" rather than complaining that he hasn't. *(praise)*
- Say, "We have 30 minutes to dress and read. When you are dressed, I will read to you. The sooner you are dressed the more time we will have." Then leave him to dress. After 25 minutes go in and help him dress if he is not ready yet. *(reward)*

Acknowledge feelings.
- "It is frustrating to interrupt yourself from playing to get dressed." *(active listening)*

Avoid the problem.
- Take his clothes to your room and let him dress there. *(removing temptation)*
- Dress him the night before in what he will wear to school. *(change schedule)*
- Say, "You may dress by yourself or I will help you." *(clarify choices)*

Consequences.
- Dress yourself by 8:50 AM or I will dress you. *(logical consequence)*
- Dress yourself by 9:00 AM or go to school in your pajamas. *(natural consequence)*

4. Plan——make and implement a plan.

I will remember that it is early to expect him to dress without being reminded. Also, I will look for what he has done and praise it rather than what he has not done.

5. Evaluate, revise and repeat.

I will try this approach for one week. If it doesn't work, I will dress him in sweats the night before so he doesn't need to change in the morning.

Screams When I Put Her in Car Seat

Situation:

Amanda (20 months) hates her car seat. She won't get in willingly. When I put her in, she screams and tries to get out. She has even opened the "child proof" buckle a couple of times. Is it really necessary to make such a big deal about car seats? Sometimes I'm tempted to let her go without.

1. Describe the problem.

Amanda refuses to get in her car seat.

2. Gather Data.

Record observations: The last six times I have tried to put her in her car seat, it has been a battle.

Is this typical for the age? Yes. Some kids dislike car seats intensely. This passes, but the interim is frustrating for both parent and child.

What behavior do you want? Since it's not safe or legal for her to ride outside the car seat, I want Amanda to get buckled into her seat without a fight.

3. Generate alternatives.

Change parent's attitude.
- Expect Amanda to fight and not worry about it. It will pass. *(change expectations)*
- Safety is important, I cannot change my value. But she doesn't need to like it. *(reaffirm values)*
- Be pleased that her persistence will make a wonderful adult trait. *(change frame of reference)*

Encourage desired behavior.
- Say, "I will watch while you get in your seat." *(attention)*
- When she is seat-belted say, "Nice sitting. Now you can be safe." *(praise)*
- Get another safety car seat and let her buckle her teddy bear in so he will be safe. When she does, say, "Nice job. Now Teddy is safe." *(redirect and praise)*
- Say, "When you are buckled in, you may have some raisins." *(reward)*
- When another adult is along, let Amanda buckle you in. And then the other adult can buckle Amanda in. When she buckles you in, say, "Good job buckling." *(attention & praise)*

Acknowledge feelings.
- "You feel confined in the car seat." *(active listening)*

Avoid the problem.
- Go shopping in the evening when her dad can take care of her. *(change schedule)*
- Get a babysitter to come in so you can go shopping alone. *(change child's activity)*
- Say, "You may get in your car seat pleasantly, or I will put you in." *(clarify choices)*

Consequences.
- Say, "No car seat, no trip." Note: before you do this, be sure the child wants to go **and** you are willing to stay home. *(logical consequence)*
- Say, "You may get in your car seat, or I will put you in." *(logical consequence)*

4. Plan——make and implement a plan.

I will explain she must use the car seat for safety reasons. Then I will praise her for cooperating.

5. Evaluate, revise, and repeat.

I will try this approach for one week. If it doesn't work, I will get a babysitter to watch her while I go on errands.

Fussy Eater

Situation:

Kevin (30 months) is a fussy eater. He is small for his size, but otherwise healthy. Sometimes he eats a lot, other times very little. He won't eat at dinner; after a few minutes he is anxious to get down. An hour later he is hungry. I worry that he is not getting what he needs. I end up letting him eat whenever he wants.

1. Describe the problem.

Kevin eats little at dinner, but snacks all evening.

2. Gather Data.

Record observations: Three days in a row he refused dinner, then had two or three snacks in the evening.

Is this typical for the age? Most children will get the nutrients they need over several days when offered nutritious food. Also, some children are natural "snackers" and do better with six planned "meals" rather than the traditional three.

What behavior do you want?
I want him to sit with us and eat a little of everything at dinner.

3. Generate alternatives.

Change parent's attitude.
- Relax. Remember that most children get what they need averaged out over several days. *(change attitude)*
- Plan for six meals a day instead of three. *(change expectations)*
- Decide it is nice to have some quiet time with my husband. *(change attitude)*

Encourage desired behavior.
- Serve only nutritious food. Sit and talk with him while he eats. *(attention)*
- Say, "Nice job. You've tried everything on your plate." *(praise)*
- Say, "When you have tried everything, you may have dessert." *(reward)*
- Involve him in meal preparation. Talk about how specific foods help his body grow. *(attention)*

Acknowledge feelings.
- "You feel bored when Daddy and I talk at the table." *(active listening)*
- "You feel frustrated when I want you to eat and you're not hungry." *(active listening)*

Avoid the problem.
- No snacks an hour or two before dinner so he will be hungry. *(removing temptation)*
- Run around the block half an hour before dinner to work up an appetite. *(change schedule)*
- Plan to eat later when Kevin is more hungry. *(change schedule)*

Alternatives—clarify choices for Kevin.
- Say, "You may eat now *or* be hungry later." *(clarify choice)*

Consequences.
- Say, "Dinner time is eating time. If you don't eat dinner, no snacks before the next meal." Then refuse to give a snack no matter how pitifully he requests. *(logical consequence)*
- Say, "If you don't finish dinner, you may have the food later as a snack." Keep the uneaten dinner and offer that if he says he is hungry. *(logical consequence)*
- Say, "If you're not hungry enough for dinner, you're not hungry enough for dessert." *(logical consequence)*

4. Plan——make and implement a plan.

I will explain that he must finish one meal before snacking. If he doesn't want his dinner, he can remain hungry until the next meal.

5. Evaluate, revise, and repeat.

I will try this approach for five days. If it doesn't work, I will try moving his dinner to an earlier time.

Bites

Situation:

Anna Marie (age 22 months) has started biting. Usually she likes playing with others, especially her little brother Eddie. But a couple of times recently she bit him or her friend Katie. She doesn't seem to be mad or anything. The kids will be playing fine, and then one of the others will cry. When I check Eddie, I find teeth marks.

1. Describe the problem.

Anna Marie is biting other children.

2. Gather Data.

Record observations: It is happening frequently—four out of five days this week. She has bitten both Eddie and my friend's little girl, Katie. She doesn't bite out of anger, because there is no disagreement or quarrelling beforehand.

Is biting typical for the age? Yes. Many preschool children bite to get attention, to express anger, or to get something they want.

What behavior do you want? I want her to touch the baby gently. If she is biting for attention, I want her to come ask me directly.

3. Generate alternatives.

Encourage desired behavior.
• Notice when she touches the baby gently and smile at her. *(attention)*
• Say, "Well done. You touched Eddie very gently." *(praise)*
• Make her own *Touch Gently* book. Look at magazines and catalogs together and hunt for pictures of gentle touching. Take some pictures of her touching gently and include them in the book. *(attention and explaining what you want)*
• Give her a sticker when she plays gently all morning. *(reward)*

Acknowledge feelings.
• "You feel ignored when I am busy for a long period." *(active listening)*

Avoid the problem.
• Don't invite your friend over for a while. *(removing temptation)*
• Invite friends over when Anna Marie is napping. *(remove temptation-change schedule)*
• Invite friends over earlier in the morning. *(change schedule)*

Alternatives—choices for Anna Marie.
• Say, "You may bite on a frozen teething ring." *(change tool)*.
• "Stroke the baby gently." *(change the activity)*
• "Play gently. I will put Eddie in a playpen when I leave the room." *(change location)*

Consequences.
• Say, "Touch gently or play alone." I will remove Anna Marie from the area if she bites. *(logical consequence)*

4. Plan——make and implement a plan.

I will explain what gentle means with a *Touch Gently* book, then I will praise her when she touches gently.

5. Evaluate, revise, and repeat.

I will try this approach for one week. If it doesn't work, I will separate the children when I leave the room.

Won't Pick Up His Toys

Situation:

I feel like a drudge. Timothy (age 3½) takes out the toys, and I put them away. I think if he gets them out, he should put them away when he is done, but it is too much trouble to get him to do it. I resent doing it alone.

1. Describe the problem.

I want help putting the toys away.

2. Gather Data.

Record observations: He has not put the toys away by himself, even once in the last five days.

Is this typical for the age? The job chart in *Pick Up Your Socks* shows the *average* age children help pick up their belongings is four, when reminded is age eight, and without being reminded is age twelve. It is reasonable to expect his help, but not to expect him to do it by himself.

What behavior do you want? I want him to help me put things away willingly.

3. Generate alternatives.

Change parent's attitude.
- Acknowledge that it is not reasonable for him to pick up all toys by himself yet. *(change expectations)*
- Decide he has to help, but he doesn't have to like it. *(change expectations)*
- Lower your standard of neatness. Decide you both can put things away once a day rather than after each use. *(change values)*
- Be glad he has a variety of toys he can use. *(change frame of reference)*
- Accept that it will take time and effort *teaching* the habit of tidiness. *(change expectations)*

Encourage desired behavior.
- Say, "You were a big help putting those toys back on the shelf." *(praise)*
- Make a game of picking up. For example, "Let's put away things with wheels ... soft toys ...books, etc." *(attention and dividing the task in small pieces)*
- Sing, "It's time to put the toys away ... " while cleaning up. When done say, "We did it!" *(praise)*
- Say, "When the toys are picked up, we will go to the park." *(reward)*

Acknowledge feelings.
- "You feel overwhelmed by the idea of putting all these toys away." *(active listening)*

Avoid the problem.
- Teach him skills to make the job easier — how to divide a task into smaller pieces and how to make a game of work. *(teach new skills)*
- Reduce the number of toys to pick up. Divide them into four groups and store three. Each week rotate the toys. *(reduce the problem)*
- Put shelves near the play area so it is convenient to put the toys away. *(restructure environment)*
- Help the child clean up at each transition (lunch time, nap, dinner). *(change schedule)*

Consequences.
- Say, "I will *help* you pick up. If you stop, I will stop." If he stops, use the next idea. *(logical consequence)*
- Say, "If you want your toys, put them away. Toys left out after bedtime will be stored for a week." Pick up the toys and put them in a large bag. Store them away for a week. *(logical consequence)*

4. Plan——make and implement a plan.

I will revise my expectations and then make picking up a game. When he helps, I will praise him.

5. Evaluate, revise, and repeat.

I will try this approach for one week. If things are not better, I will store toys not picked up.

Fights Diaper Changes

Situation:

William (18 months) hates having his diaper changed. Sometimes he will even hit me to stop me from changing his diaper.

1. Describe the problem.

William resists diaper changes.

2. Gather Data.

Record observations: Four out of the six times I changed William's diapers he tried to stop me.

Is this typical for the age? Many toddlers resist diaper change.

What behavior do you want? I want him to cooperate or to tell me he doesn't want them changed.

3. Generate alternatives.

Change parent's attitude.

- Expect a hassle. Don't get sucked into his anger or frustration. *(change expectations)*
- Tell yourself, "This too will pass. No one wears a diaper when they graduate from high school." *(change frame of reference)*

Encourage desired behavior.

- Sing or play games together while you change the diaper. *(attention)*
- If he says, "No" when you go to diaper him, say, "I'm glad you used words." *(praise)*
- When he cooperates say, "You stayed very still. I'm proud of you." *(praise)*
- Together, make a picture book of "Ways I like my diaper changed." *(attention)*

Acknowledge feelings.

- Say, "You feel angry because you don't want to have your diapers changed." *(active listening)*

Avoid the problem.

- Have special toys (like a mirror or music box) that he can *only* use while getting his diaper changed. *(add to the environment)*
- Place William so that if he kicks, he can't kick you. *(change environment)*

Alternatives—choices for William.

- Say, "You may choose how I diaper you. You can lie down or stand up." *(change activity)*
- Say, "You may choose where I change your diaper — living room floor or bathroom." *(change location)*
- Say, "You may choose when I change your diaper — now or in five minutes." *(change time)*

Consequences.

- "You can lie still for diapering and be done quickly, or you can wiggle and it will take much longer." *(logical consequence)*

4. Plan——make and implement a plan.

I will begin by asking him where, when, and how he would like to be diapered. When he lies still, I will praise him and sing with him.

5. Evaluate, revise, and repeat.

I will try this approach for one week. If it doesn't work, I will buy some special "diapering toys" to interest him during changing.

Trouble Getting My Kids to Bed at Night.

Situation:

I dread bedtime at my house. I'm tired and the kids (Marie 2½ and Martin 4½) are rowdy and uncooperative. No matter how many times I remind them, they don't get ready for bed. When I say, "Now is the time to go to bed," Marie starts to cry and Martin runs and hides. They don't do anything until I scream at them. When I finally get them each in their own room, they cry and say they are scared. I feel angry and guilty. I want them to go to bed at a reasonable time so I have some time to myself.

1. Describe the problem.

The children ignore my reminders and use several delaying tactics.

2. Gather Data.

Record observations: Four nights this week it has been a major battle. **Note:** It would be helpful to know what is different about the days that work better. Are you more patient? ...kids more tired? ... you had a stressful day? ... restful day? ... you started bedtime earlier or later?

Is this typical for the age? Many children resist going to bed — some because they are not tired, — some because they are overtired, and some because they are having fun and don't want it to stop. Some children need firm (not harsh) guidance in developing good sleep habits.

What behavior do you want?
I want my kids to go to bed promptly and peacefully.

3. Generate alternatives.

Change parent's attitude.
- Accept that bedtime will be a hassle. Start being firm *before* you run out of patience and energy. *(change expectations)*
- Let the children sleep together. Worldwide, most children sleep with parents or other children. *(change expectations)*
- Decide your kids have to go to bed promptly, but they don't need to like it. *(change expectations)*
- Decide that your kids don't need bedtimes, they can go to sleep when they are tired. *(change values)*
- See the children's reluctance to go to bed as an indication of the fun they have, rather than that they are "out to get you." *(change your frame of reference)*
- Be glad your children enjoy each other and want to spend time together. *(change your frame of reference)*
- Figure out how much sleep your child really needs. Some kids don't need as much as parents wish they needed. *(change expectations)*

Encourage desired behavior.
- Make a game of getting ready for bed. For example, play Simon Says, Follow the Leader, or adapt the Hokey-Pokey song. *(attention)*
- When they behave appropriately, say, "I appreciate your help getting in your pajamas." *(praise)*
- Say, "If you are in bed before the timer rings, I will read you an extra story." *(reward)*
- Say, "I have the next 20 minutes to help you get in bed. If you are in bed before the timer rings I will read you an extra story." *(reward)*

Acknowledge feelings.
- Say, "Sometimes you feel lonely/scared when you sleep alone." *(active listening)*
- Say, "Sometimes it is hard to go to bed when you are having so much fun." *(active listening)*

Continued on the next page

Avoid the problem.

- Notice how the better evenings are different from the hard ones. Restructure things like the better days. *(removing temptation)*
- If you need more personal time than you are getting after bedtime, rearrange things so that you get some free time earlier in the day. Trade babysitting with a friend, join a babysitting cooperative, hire a "mother's helper" — an older child to entertain the kids in your house while you are home. *(change schedule)*
- Develop a bedtime ritual. Always use it, but do not allow the ritual to be extended very much. *(establishing a schedule)*
- Say, "You don't have to go to sleep, but you must stay in bed quietly." *(clarify expectations)*
- Start earlier, before you lose patience. *(change schedule)*

Alternatives —choices for Marie and Martin.

- Say, "You may look at books in bed quietly or listen to the tape recorder." *(choice of activity)*
- Say, "You may sleep in your bed or in a sleeping bag on the floor." *(choice of location)*

Consequences.

- Say, "You may read in bed quietly, or you can lie in bed with the light off." **Note:** for children afraid of the dark, you may need to leave a night light on instead of the overhead light. *(logical consequence)*
- "Bedtime is 7:30, it's time to get ready at 7:00. If you are not in bed at 7:30 tonight then you must start earlier tomorrow." *(logical consequence)*
- Say, "Marie, you may go to bed in Martin's room quietly or go to bed in your room. If you get out of bed or are noisy, I will know you have chosen to sleep in your room." **Note:** If they are noisy you must remove Marie from the room, even if they promise to do better. Say, "I'm glad you will rest quietly if I leave you. You will get another chance to try tomorrow night." *(logical consequence)*

4. Plans—make and implement a plan.

I will try to notice what is different between the easy days and the hard days. In the meantime I will make a game of dressing and give them attention for dressing.

5. Evaluate, revise, and repeat.

I will try this approach for five nights. If it doesn't work, I will find a "mother's helper" to come in three days a week for a month so I don't feel so used up and resentful.

Won't Sit Still

Situation:
Andrew (age 3) won't sit still. He won't sit still for dinner, in the doctor's office, or at church. I get embarrassed in public and frustrated at home. I'm at my wit's end.

1. Describe the problem.
Andrew won't sit still.

2. Gather Data.

Record observations: On the bus ride this morning, he wanted to run up and down the aisle. At the doctor's office, he wanted to know what everyone was doing rather than sit still. At my Aunt Cathy's apartment, he wanted to explore rather than color or play with the puzzles she provided. The longest he can be still is for two or three minutes.

Is this typical for the age? It depends. Three factors affect what is reasonable: (1) the length of time you expect the child to be still, (2) the temperament of the child, and (3) what activities are available. Three year olds can usually sit between 5 and 15 minutes if they have something to interest them. However, very active children may have trouble sitting still for five minutes. All children find it easier to sit quietly when they have interesting activities.

What behavior do you want? I want Andrew to sit still for ten minutes.

3. Generate alternatives.

Change parent's attitude.
- Aim for 5-6 minutes — 10 may be too long for an active temperament. *(change expectations)*
- Decide, "I am glad he has lots of energy," and help him use it constructively. *(change point of view)*

Encourage desired behavior.
- Pay lots of attention while he is sitting. *(attention)*
- Say, "I'm pleased you are sitting quietly. I know it's hard for you." *(praise)*
- Give him a sticker for every five minutes he is quiet. *(reward)*

Acknowledge feelings.
- Say, "It is boring to sit and wait." *(active listening)*
- Say, "I get embarrassed when you run around, because it disturbs other people." *(I-message)*

Avoid the problem.
- Bring truck, ball, or activity he can move about with a little when he uses it. *(enrich the environment)*
- Bring activities to do while sitting. *(enrich the environment)*
- Go running for several minutes before going inside to sit. *(reduce energy)*
- Schedule trips in the early morning before he gets restless. *(change schedule)*
- Get a babysitter and go without Andrew. *(change schedule)*

Alternatives—choices for Andrew.
- "You may play quietly with the cars *(change tool)* or run on the sidewalk." *(change the activity)*

Consequences.
- "You may play quietly inside, or wait in the hall (or other dull place)." *(logical consequence)*

4. Plan——make and implement a plan.

I will remember he is active and has difficulty sitting quietly for more than a few minutes. I will give him attention and praise when he does sit still.

5. Evaluate, revise, and repeat.

I will try this approach for two weeks. If it doesn't work, I will try rewarding him for sitting still.

Appendix Two:
Summary Sheets for Ten Tools

The following sheets summarize the material in the text. Copy the ones you need and post them where you can review them frequently.

Thirty-one Tools

This is a list of the tools described in *Without Spanking or Spoiling*. These tools can be adapted for various challenges. No one tool works equally well for everyone or in every situation — so experiment. Find what works for you.

A Better Way Summary
Described on page 70

What
A Better Way is a simple form of negotiation. It helps you and your child find a solution that works for *both* of you. There are three parts: a statement of what you want; a statement of what you believe the child wants; and a request for new ideas.

When
A Better Way can be used when you and your child are in a power struggle. Use this tool *only* if you are willing to accept a different position.

Procedure
1. State what you want in a pleasant voice. Get on the same level as your child. *"My way is ... "*
2. State the child's position. *"Your way is ... "*
3. Ask for ideas that work for both of you. Explain what *A Better Way* is. *"What is a better way? A Better Way is an idea we both like."*
4. Consider the child's suggestion and try to make it work. If you can't, explain why you can't agree and suggest the closest thing you can think of to his or her idea. In the begining you may find it helpful to accept some marginal ideas so your child gets the feel of working together.

How *not* to do it
Dad picks up the newspaper and heads for the sofa to rest while he reads.

Cassie: Daddy, Daddy, Daddy, play space with me.

Dad: Later, Cassie. I want to read the paper first. (He steps closer to the sofa.)

Cassie: (Grabs his leg.) Please. Please, please, please.

Dad: Not now! I want to read.

Cassie: Ple-e-e-a-se, Daddy.

Dad: (Looks down at Cassie.) My way is I read. Your way is I play space. What's a better way? What's an idea we both will like.

Cassie: You play train with me.

Dad: (Looking down at her) Cassie, I don't want to play now. What's *A Better Way*?

Cassie: I don't know.

How to do it
Dad picks up the newspaper and heads for the sofa to rest while he reads.

Cassie: Daddy, Daddy, Daddy, play space with me.

Dad: Later, Cassie. I want to read the paper the paper first. (He steps closer to the sofa.)

Cassie: (Grabs his leg.) Please. Please, please, please.

Dad: (Dad kneels down by Cassie.) Cassie, my way is I read now. Your way is I play space now. What is a better way? A Better Way is an idea we both will like.

Cassie: You play train with me.

Dad: Can I be a passenger on your train and read?

Cassie: Yes.

Dad: Great idea. Where shall I sit?

Active Listening Summary
Described on pages 41-44

What
Active listening is a technique for helping another person clarify her feelings (so she can solve her own problems).

When
When the other person indicates, by what she says or does, that she has a problem.

How
Active listening reflects both the feeling and the content of the other person's message (both verbal and nonverbal). Active listening avoids asking questions, reasoning, giving advice, or encouraging a course of action.

How *not* to do it
(Mother and daughter driving to the babysitter's):
Daughter: I don't wan-na go a Susie's house.
Mother: You don't want to go to Susie's house?
Daughter: I don't wan-na go a Susie's house.
Mother: Why not? You always have fun there.
Daughter: (louder) I don't wan-na go a Susie's house.
Mother: Why are you afraid to go to Susie's?
Daughter: I wan-na be wif you.
Mother: But honey, you know I have to go to work.
Daughter: (crying loudly) I wan-na be wif you. I wan-na be wif you.
Mother: Just calm down. Crying won't make it any better.

How to do it
(Mother and daughter driving to the babysitter's):
Daughter: I don't wan-na go a Susie's house.
Mother: (groping) You are sad we are going to Susie's house.
Daughter: (louder) I don't wan-na go to Susie's house.
Mother: You want to stay with me.
Daughter: (calmer) Yes, I wan-na be wif you.
Mother: Okay, I'll stay with you for a little bit at Susie's house.
Daughter: 'For you go?
Mother: Before I go.

Note
Active listening can also be used to reflect or clarify happy, joyous feelings. If a child seems to dwell on the unpleasant side of life, active listening happy, successful experiences may help.

Consequences Summary
Described on pages 82-85

What

A "consequence" is a technique for use with unacceptable behavior. It gives the child responsibility for the results of his own actions.

Natural consequences are the direct results (or consequences) of the child's own actions. The natural consequence of playing in the snow without mittens is cold hands.

Logical consequences are the results (consequences) of the child's actions that are provided by an adult. A logical consequence of hitting someone is being removed from him.

Requirements for a consequence

A consequence must — • be related to the unacceptable behavior.
                           • occur every time the unacceptable behavior does.
                           • be acceptable to the parent.

How *not* to do it

A. *To a child who refuses to finish lunch.* "If you don't finish your sandwich, you cannot watch Sesame Street this afternoon." When the child refuses to eat, he is not permitted to watch the television. (The consequence is not related to the behavior.)

B. *To a child who is slow dressing.* "Sara, if you are not ready for school when the ride comes, you will have to stay home." When the ride comes, Sara only needs to put on her socks, shoes, and coat. She pleads with mother to help her. Mother helps her finish dressing and lets her go to school. (The consequence did not happen every time.)

C. *To a child who refuses to clean up toys.* "Brian, if there are any toys left on the floor tonight, I will throw them all away." Brian picks up most of them, but leaves a couple. Mother picks up the remaining toys and puts them away. After all, she can't afford to go out and buy new toys. (The consequence was not really acceptable to the parent.)

How to do it

A. *To a child who refuses to finish lunch.* "Chuck, please eat enough to last until dinner. We are going to the park and there will be no snacks." He does not eat much. Later in the afternoon, Chuck says he is really hungry and wants an ice cream cone on the way home. Mother replies, "I'll bet you are really hungry. We won't be eating until daddy gets home. Would you like me to play a game with you?" (If she gives him a snack, she will prevent him from experiencing the results (hunger) of his decision.)

B. *To a child who is slow dressing.* "If you are not ready when your ride comes, Sara, you will have to stay home." When the ride comes, she needs socks, shoes, and a coat. Sara pleads for Mom to help her. Instead of assisting her, Mother goes out and tells the driver that Sara is not going to preschool today.

C. *To a child who refuses to clean up his toys.* "Any toys left on the floor this evening will disappear for several days." That evening Mother picks up the toys that are left out and puts them in a box that is out of sight. At least she will not have to pick up those same toys for a while.

                                       Without Spanking or Spoiling

Ignoring Summary
Described on page 78

What
Extinction (ignoring) is a technique to reduce or eliminate unacceptable behavior. When you ignore behavior, you pay NO attention (in words or actions) to that behavior.

When
Use extinction on behavior that is not serious (dangerous or destructive) such as quarreling, interrupting, or "bugging."

Procedure
1. Define what behavior you want to decrease.
2. Decide whether you can tolerate the behavior while the child is learning to control it.
   - If so, you can use extinction as a technique.
   - If not, use another technique.
3. When the behavior occurs, continue what you are doing. Do not look at or talk to the child.
4. Decide what you WANT the child to do instead. (If both parents are involved, they should agree.)
5. When the child finally does the desired behavior, praise and/or reinforce the child.

How *not* to do it
Mother is talking with a neighbor. Cindy repeatedly interrupts the conversation by calling "Mom," again and again, and pulling at her arm.

Mom: I'm talking, Cindy.

Cindy: Mom, Mom. (In a louder voice)

Mom: Be quiet!

Cindy: Mom! (Pulls on Mom's arm)

Mom: Stop pulling at my arm! (Pushes Cindy away)

Cindy: (Starts yelling at Mom in a loud voice, stamping her feet, and pushing Mom away from the neighbor.)

Mom: What's the matter, Cindy?

How to do it
Mom decides to ignore Cindy's interruptions. She tells the neighbor that she wants the child to learn to wait and asks the neighbor not to look at or pay attention to Cindy's interruptions. Conversation continues between Mom and the neighbor. Eventually Cindy stops pulling at Mom's arm and stands quietly, looking confused. When there is a break in the conversation, Mom says, "Good waiting, Cindy!" and then attends to Cindy's problem.

Note
1. Ignoring may be very difficult, and at times it may be necessary to leave the area where the child is.
2. Remember — any attention to unacceptable behavior will only reinforce it and probably increase its frequency.

Modifying the Environment Summary
Described on pages 81-82

What
Modifying the environment is a technique which involves altering the surroundings to encourage or discourage certain behavior.

When
The technique of modifying the environment is used when a child's surroundings are unsafe, when a particular situation usually results in conflicts, or when making changes can make the child's or parent's life easier.

How
The environment can be modified by adding to it, limiting it, or changing things around.

Adding to the environment

Examples

Enrichment	Introducing materials or activities that engage the child's interest.	•provide a new book •demonstrate new use of an old toy •take crayons and paper when you go to the doctors office
Enlargement	Broadening the area in which the child may play.	•trip to the park •going out in the back yard

Limiting the environment

Reduce	Reducing a stimulus (activity) or removing a physical stimulus (item).	•no roughhousing •removing crayons •turning off the TV
Restrict	Restricting certain activities to certain areas.	•ride trike in the basement •playdough at the table •loud noises outdoors

Changing the environment

Simplifying	Making it easier for the child to function independently and effectively.	•step stool in the kitchen •plate with rim •low towel rack
Rearranging	Displaying or storing items in the home to encourage or discourage certain behavior.	•store poisons up high and locked •put toys on low shelf for easy access •have a coat rack by the door

Without Spanking or Spoiling

Positive Reinforcement Summary

Described on pages 52-55

What

Positive reinforcement is a technique used to increase the frequency of desired behavior.

How

A positive reinforcer increases the behavior that immediately precedes it, and can be anything a child wants or needs.

Procedure

1. Decide on the specific behavior that you want. Be sure that the child is capable of performing it.
2. Decide on an appropriate reinforcer. (Something your child wants or needs.)
3. Watch your child carefully. Reinforce the desired behavior or attempts to perform it.
4. Ignore failures to perform the desired behavior.
5. When the desired behavior becomes a habit, decrease the frequency of reinforcement.

How *not* to do it

1. Mother wants Peter to hang his coat up.
2. She decides to give him a star as a positive reinforcer.
3. The next time Peter comes in, his mother is on the phone. She watches him make a half-hearted attempt to hang the coat up, before he drops it on the floor. Several minutes later, when she is finished with the call, she goes to Peter and says, "I told you to hang your coat up when you come in. I want it done now!"
4. The next day Peter comes in and drops his coat on the floor. Mother goes after him immediately and reminds him to hang it up.

How to do it

1. Mother wants Peter to hang up his coat. She installs a hook low enough for him to use easily.
2. She decides that since Peter likes smiley faces, she will give him a smiley face sticker when he hangs up his coat.
3. The next time Peter comes in, she is on the phone. She immediately excuses herself and gets a smiley face so she will be ready to reinforce an attempt. Peter makes a half-hearted attempt to hang his coat up. Mother tells him, "I am so glad you tried to hang your coat up. Here is a smiley face," and she helps him hang it up.
4. Later, when Peter comes in again, he drops his coat on the hall floor. Mother says nothing. But she reinforces him the next time he remembers to hang it up.
5. Several days later, when Peter is remembering well, his mother lets Peter hang up his coat without reinforcement. She is careful to be available to reinforce him the next time he hangs his coat up and tells him, "Peter, I am so glad you hung your coat up. I don't have to reward you each time any more." From then on she gradually increases the length of time between the reinforcements.

Praise Summary
Described on pages 59-60

What
Praise is a way of saying, "I like what you did!" The message can be a word, a phrase, a gesture, or a facial expression. Praise makes the other person feel pride, joy, or respect.

When or Where
When you see a child doing something that you want to encourage, praise it! You might praise cooperative play, thoughtfulness, going potty in the toilet, treating the baby gently, tasting all the food served, trying something that is difficult, etc.

To be effective, the praise must be specific (indicate what you like), immediate, and sincere.

How *not* to praise
The positive value of praise can be lost if the praise is coupled with a negative comparison.

A. "For a little girl, you did very well." (The child thinks, "I'm really too small to do a really good job.")

B. "I'm glad you remembered to hang up your clothes today; I hope you won't forget tomorrow." (The child thinks, "I'm stupid to forget so much.")

C. (To a child unsuccessfully trying to put some preschool Legos together) "I see you are having trouble with the Legos again. Here is your train; you can use it very well." (The child thinks, "I'd better stick to something I can do well.")

How to praise
Praise is most effective when is related to the event, not the child's character.

A. "I'm glad you shared your blocks with Amy. She was feeling left out, and now she is having fun."

B. "Wow! You put your clothes away nicely this evening. Your shoes are in the closet, and your dirty clothes are all in the clothes basket."

C. (To a child unsuccessfully trying to put some preschool Legos together) "I'm glad to see you trying to put the Legos together. It is really hard to fit them together, but you are trying."

Setting Limits Summary
Described on pages 47-48

What

Setting limits clarifies for the child both the behavior that you want and the consequences if the child resists your request. There are three parts: a clear rule or request; an explanation of choices; and immediate assisted compliance (follow through).

When

Set limits when your child's behavior is inappropriate or dangerous.

Procedure

1. Think the situation through —
   • What do you want the child *to do* instead of what he is doing?
   • What will you *really* do if the child defies or ignores you? No empty threats here. If you know you will back down, do not try to set the limit.
2. Set the limit. Get the child's attention. Tell the child the rule in a pleasant manner and wait a minute for compliance.
3. Explain the choices. Tell him what he may do instead of what he was doing and what will happen if he continues to ignore the request.
4. Assist the child to comply. Pick the child up or physically "help" him to do as required. If the child begins to comply as you approach, continue to help anyway.

How *not* to do it

Mom: Cathy, it's time to go home. Please get ready. (Nothing happens.) Cathy, put your books down and get ready to go. (No change.) I said, It's time to go, put your coat on. (No response.) Cathy Lynn, do you hear me? If you don't put your coat on right now, you will be sorry. (Still no response. Mom gets up, gets Cathy's coat and takes it to her.)

Cathy: Okay. (As she picks up her coat. However, as soon as her mother sits down she drops her coat, and picks up her book.)

Mom: (Notices Cathy has stopped and returns.) Can't you do anything yourself?

Cathy: I do it. (She picks up her coat. When Mom's attention wanders she puts it down again.)

Mom: (Notices Cathy has stopped again.) Can't you do anything by yourself? (Mom angrily helps Cathy into the coat.)

How to do it

Mom: Cathy, it's time to go home. Please put your coat on. (Nothing happens. Mom gets on eye level with Cathy.) Cathy, It's time to go. Do you want to put your coat on yourself, or do you want me to help you? (Still no action. Mom starts to put the coat on Cathy.) I see you want me to help you.

Cathy: No. No. I can do it. (She tries to take the coat.)

Mom: I know you can. This time you chose for me to help you. Next time you can choose to do it alone. (Mom continues to help her put the coat on.)

Substitution Summary
Described on pages 79-81

What
Substitution involves replacing an inappropriate activity with an acceptable form of the same activity. It follows the idea that the activity is not bad, but inappropriate. (Substitution differs from distraction in that the activity is encouraged.)

When
Substitution is used when a child's activity is unsafe, annoying, or antisocial, but can be redirected to an acceptable form.

Procedure
1. Decide what is "wrong" with the activity.
2. Choose a substitute "tool" or "location."
3. Calmly and firmly make the substitution. (You can replace the "tool" or move the child to the new "location.")
4. Explain briefly why you are making the substitution.
5. Encourage the child to continue the activity.

How *not* to do it
A. Mother sees Peg in the living room drinking grape juice. She takes the glass away and says, "Shame on you for drinking in here. Here's a book, look at it!"
B. Mother sees Tommy making a peanut butter sandwich with a sharp kitchen knife. Mother takes away the knife and says, "No, no. Tommy is too little," and then makes the sandwich for him.

How to do it
A. Daughter Peg is drinking her grape juice standing on the beige living room rug.
  1. Mother is afraid Peg will spill some grape juice on the rug and stain it.
  2. Mother decides to change "the location" and move Peg to the kitchen.
  3. Mother moves Peg to the kitchen where spills can be wiped up easier.
  4. Mother explains, "We drink juice in the kitchen or at the table so it is easier to clean up."
  5. The message Peg gets is, "It is okay to drink grape juice in the kitchen or in chairs."

B. Mother sees two-year-old Tommy trying to make a peanut butter sandwich with a sharp kitchen knife.
  1. The knife is sharp.
  2. Mother will substitute a table knife. *(changing the tool)*
  3. She removes the sharp knife and replaces it with the table knife.
  4. Mother explains, "This is a sharp knife for cutting; this is a table knife for making sandwiches."
  5. Mother scoops some peanut butter on the table knife and gives it to Tommy so that he can finish his sandwich.

Time-Out Summary
Described on pages 85-90

What
A time-out (T.O.) is used to interrupt unacceptable behavior by removing the child from the "scene of the action." A T.O. is a calming device, *not* a punishment.

When and Where
Use T.O.'s for stopping inappropriate behavior before it reaches oppressive or assaultive proportions, or for serious violations of your family's rules.

The T.O. should be short enough that the child has many chances to go back to the original situation and learn acceptable behavior (a minute or less for young children).

Procedure
Before using a time-out, see if your child understands the concepts of "wait" and "quiet" (usually occurs between 2½ and 3½). Then choose an appropriate location.

First few times:
1. Explain a time-out to the child.
2. Explain when a T.O. will be used.
3. Walk the child through the steps (when a rule is broken).
4. Time the quiet time only (not whining or crying).
5. Tell the child the T.O. is over when the time is up.
6. Return the child to the situation and reinforce appropriate behavior.

How *not* to do it
Tommy's provoking ("egging-on") of Joey at the dinner table leads to silliness and interrupts Mom and Dad's conversation. Mother pleads, "Come on, boys, eat your supper. If you finish a little more, you can have some cake." Father threatens, "Shut up and eat, or you'll go to your room for the rest of the night." The behavior continues and father drags Tommy to the basement steps shouting, "Take a time-out right here! Sit here until you have settled down!" Tommy blasts back, "I didn't do it, Joey did!" Father argues, "I don't care what he did or what you did. Now sit down and shut up!" The argument continues until Tommy whines, "O.K., O.K., I'll eat now." At this, his father lets him return with a command to, "Behave as you're supposed to!" Mother places dessert at his place and soon the boys are bickering again.

How to do it
The first time Mother or Father sees or senses silliness at the table, either parent tells the child to sit on the basement stairs. Sometimes Tommy complains, but he stays in the T.O. Sometimes he peeks around the corner to provoke his brother Joey. Mother and Father ignore Tommy, telling him only *once* more that the T.O. begins when he is quiet. When he has been quiet about a minute, Father goes to Tommy and says, "Tommy, I sent you to a time-out on the stairs because you can't eat supper and be silly at the same time. You took your T.O. so you can come back now and eat." As he picks up his knife to butter his bread, Mother follows up with, "That's good, Tommy. You've settled down now."

Index (**Bold** page numbers are summary sheets)

Without Spanking or Spoiling